The case f
Independ
Developer

Roger Zogolovitch

r the

nt

Artifice
books on architecture

solidspace

Roger Zogolovitch is an architect and developer
and founder of Solidspace, independent developers
working exclusively on 'gap sites'. Inside each
of their projects is an open-plan split-level form
that provides space to eat, live and work. Volume
is generated by this split-floor plate, giving
the impression of spaciousness. Each project,
undertaken with collaborating architects, pursues
a consistent approach to a sculptural form of
development, modelling volumes internally and
externally to suit the occupier and the city with
imagination and equality.

For my mother, Fay, who, had she still been alive, would have surely bought every copy.

© 2015 Artifice books on architecture, the architect(s) and
author(s). All rights reserved.

Artifice books on architecture
10A Acton Street
London WC1X 9NG

Telephone +44 (0)20 7713 5097
Fax +44 (0)20 7713 8682
sales@artificebooksonline.com
www.artificebooksonline.com

All opinions expressed within this publication are those of the
authors and not necessarily of the publisher.

Designed by Abrahams
British Library Cataloguing-in-Publication Data
A CIP record for this book is available from the British Library

ISBN 978 1 908967 68 8

No part of this publication may be reproduced, stored in a
retrieval system, or transmitted, in any form or by any means,
electronic, mechanical, photocopying, recording, or otherwise,
without prior permission of the publisher.

Every effort has been made to trace the copyright holders,
but if any have been inadvertently overlooked the necessary
arrangements will be made at the first opportunity.

Artifice books on architecture is an environmentally responsible
company. *Shouldn't we all be developers?* is printed on sustainably
sourced paper.

Contents

Foreword: Paul Finch	8
Introduction	12
Chapter 1: Planning	30
Chapter 2: Land	44
Chapter 3: Design	56
Chapter 4: Brand	68
Chapter 5: Money	80
Chapter 6: Interiors	94
Chapter 7: Materials	108
Chapter 8: The Developer and the State	120
Chapter 9: Case studies	138
Glossary	172
Endnotes	178
Further references	182
Acknowledgements	186
Index	187

Foreword by Paul Finch

Impresarios succeed by understanding people — and life

Roger Zogolovitch is an architect who develops houses and apartments. This treatise, on how to address our acute housing shortage, is part political manifesto, part provocation for supporters of the status quo; it is not a cynical exposition from an ideologue of the free-market homebuilding lobby, but a heartfelt plea from an idealist (and some would say romantic), committed to the challenge of housing *all* our people in decent dwellings.

It is a sign of our times that we have abandoned as public policy the desirability of supplying well-designed homes for ordinary people. This publication is a clarion call for the proper provision of a basic human requirement. It would have had little impact 40 years ago, since it would have been an automatic assumption that such provision should be made, though the reasons for the abandonment of the 'predict and provide' philosophy, which served us well for generations after 1945, are not the subject matter of this publication. The consequences of that abandonment certainly are.

Questions are raised about a series of connected issues: land, planning, finance, branding and materials, as well as architecture and design. They prompt thoughtful observations from the author, followed by analyses, propositions and imagined outcomes, should his strategies for improvement be introduced by any concerned government.

Housing shortages across the UK make this publication both timely and worrying. The ideas it contains have been discussed and promoted by the author and a few others within the design and development fraternity for many years. So far, however, translation of these ideas, about both design and supply, has failed to lodge in the minds of the politicians whose support will be crucial if they are to gain traction. Let's hope they listen harder.

A cynic might note that the inability to deliver UK housing numbers is in inverse proportion to the number of speeches made by elected officers and planning officials, claiming that everything is under control. Everything is not under control, unless you take the view that a desirable housing market is one designed to attract absentee overseas investors; encourage buy-to-let speculators to price out first-time buyers struggling to find mortgage finance because of banking market failure; and make millionaires out of existing home-owners through failure to build for their children and grandchildren.

The Zogolovitch proposition to address this, put simply, is to increase supply by encouraging an increase in providers through more permissive and rational legislative regimes. His subject areas range across the gamut of housing market issues, which is only appropriate since the inter-connectedness of finance, land, design and construction can often be underplayed. (The exploration of the split section and the joys of concrete, through his Solidspace development company, would make a book in themselves.)

His perfect world would be one in which independent developers permitted to undertake housing projects, by virtue of their financial and design credentials, would consult with residents before building small-scale projects in large numbers, using As-of-Right development benefits to speed everything up.

This is a reversion to a condition which existed (sort of) before the introduction of the 1947 Town & Country Planning Act, that is to say a world in which development was regarded as desirable rather than suspicious, and in which the introduction of more dwellings was assumed to be a social good rather than a threat to conservation areas. House-builders knew their market, and if that was what people wanted, the local authority would do what it could to help.

Under the imagined regime described in the pages that follow, the punishment for producing poor-quality development would be demolition within 30 years of completion, an 'x-listing' system which would allow the replacement of the inadequate, following compulsory purchase/demolition.

This is a take-it-or-leave-it detail which should not divert from the fundamental aspirations in the Zogolovitch manifesto: make the market easier for smaller independent suppliers; give good guys a faster journey through planning; stop delaying decent development through trifling regulation of details which are matters for the market rather than planning committees; and view the issue of supply as being more significant than fiddling with the design proposals of qualified professionals.

The title of this publication, *Shouldn't we all be developers?* is a cri de coeur from the sort of individual much admired in British culture: the sort of individual who thinks that if enough of the small guys got together, they could make a better fist of things than the big battalions who seem to dominate ideas about where and how we should live, and what it should look like. The big battalions, for a variety of reasons, aren't going to provide the numbers. Others are needed to take on the job.

Generations to come will find it astonishing that we have agonised for so long over the matter of fundamental social provision that housing represents. It is often said that if you are in a hole, the correct thing to do is to stop digging. What this publication suggests is that we should keep digging, literally and metaphorically, not to create endless Kensington basements, but to extricate ourselves from a political, financial and planning quagmire, an enemy both of architecture and a notion of social equity.

Paul Finch is editorial director of the Architects' Journal *and* Architectural Review *and programme director of the World Architecture Festival.*

Making Developm as Art

12 Shouldn't we all be developers?

Introduction

Imagine a supermarket with its shelves 60 per cent empty. Consider driving into the petrol station expecting to fill your tank with 60 litres of fuel only to be offered 25, or turning up at the ATM only to receive £40 for every £100 of your money requested. This is rationing. This is what it means when the number of housing completions in London to September 2014 were 19,700 new homes rather than the 50,000 we need.[1]

The effect, unsurprisingly, has pushed the average price of a home to £504,000, 14 times our average incomes.[2] House prices rose by 25 per cent between June 2013 and June 2014.[3]

London growth and domination, described by the late Sir Peter Hall in 2000 as a "polycentric mega-city region" now covers more than 20 per cent of England's land area and contains close to 40 per cent of its entire population.[4] In 2014, Greater London's population reached 8.6 million with the current prediction for the population by 2031 to be 10 million.[5]

This is the crisis where the continuing success of London is now threatened by a famine in housing and misalliance of supply and demand. The theme of this book is simply to examine ways to create more housing on sites in the centres of our cities.

I trained and practiced as an architect. 30 years ago I changed career and became a developer. I had become frustrated as an architect. I decided to take on a wider responsibility for my work. I wanted to be in control of the projects that I undertook and I wanted to be able to engage with all aspects of making buildings, not just their design.

My work has been making regeneration projects in run down and underused parts of the city. I use London as my example because it is here I have spent my whole career, where I was born, went to school, university and where I make development slowly, site by site.

I walk the streets in search of development potential in the midst of the tight urban fabric. I enjoy the excitement of discovery. I imagine how the existing might transform into something new.

I scan spaces next to railways, behind houses, around factories and warehouses to spot opportunities for redevelopment. I call these "gap sites". I see them as patterns of solid and void. I read the city as a constantly shifting pattern of these solids and voids. The solid is the built form and the void the spaces between.

These voids are made up of gardens, yards, roads, streets and the sky — all space outside the built form as seen from both inside and outside those buildings. Proliferation is the art of finding imaginative ways of increasing the solid without damaging the void. The form that such a development should take in the city is an art not a science. It is the visualisation of what volume might be built in this particular context.

"Development as Art" is the name that I have coined to describe this form of building which is driven by my imagination. I take full responsibility for every part of the process; from concept, detailed design, fire regulations, planning, drainage, kitchen and bathroom layouts all fitting around spaces and volumes that make up the development. I inspect and direct each discipline, from the marketing to funding to building and planning. The entire process of development is original and authentic. I take responsibility for being the champion. I want to remake parts of the city and leave them better. I have found this approach more akin to directing a film or creating a restaurant. It is a close and intense engagement employing a team of different disciplines all looking to the developer to lead, to be decisive and to drive the projects on to their realisation.

The history of development has always engaged me. Even as a child, I listened to my grandfather's tales of the esoteric but fascinating account of sale and leaseback and the building up of Odeon cinemas surrounded as they were by parades of shops. A growing understanding of the history of development has been an essential skill to fulfil my ambition of making good projects that connect intelligently with their past — buildings that sit comfortably in their surroundings.

My developments deserve critical review, they have quality, are made with a passion and are driven by originality. It should not be a surprise, although it invariably is, that development can and should be a positive contribution to the city. I am asking you to move away from your preconception and to believe in that possibility.

Examining the more intricate mechanics of development reveals the connections between each part of a wider development process. I describe them as cogs that must interlock with each other to deliver projects. In every chapter, I explore simple adjustments that could make that whole machine run better.

Report after report dwells on our long-term failure to provide homes and seem always to offer only the very wide-ranging strategic solutions. What intrigues me is the opportunity for change without needing a dramatic political shift. I fear that the intractable nature of these big scale interventions return us regrettably to the status quo.

In the chapters of this book I look at the individual elements that make up the developer's world rather like a cook book looks at courses on a menu. My headings of planning, land, design, brand, money, interiors, materials and the state are all subsets of the wider connected machine of development. They are each a discipline in their own right but are all interlinked. Development needs land or building, but once you have that you can't build without planning consent, which is driven by policy and design. Design defines product, while brand is the part of the process that engages the wider public and bridges the trust between consumer and producer. Money acts as the fuel that powers the machinery of development. Interiors are the touchstone of our personality and aspiration. Materials represent the solidity, the mass that makes the structure and the state which, as remarked by Peter Hall after 1947, "effectively nationalised development rights" need to become engaged.[6]

Nimbyism is blamed for people's resistance to change, particularly where gap sites drive redevelopment close to neighbouring properties. It is perhaps a peculiarly English trait of conservatism towards the existing and a natural fear of change. It is more of a concern in a locality where the majority of residents are long-term, middle class and middle aged. I suggest different mechanisms to improve trust between the developer and these communities.

As an independent developer you need a combination of skill, initiative and imagination steering projects through this complex machine. Watching and waiting at each rotation of a particular cog for the gear to drop and move on to the next. There is something frustrating about trying to make the project a success but finding resistance at every turn. I have in this book sought to find the simplest adjustments to help smooth this self-organising system and increase its output.

Development's great historical strength was one of individual enterprise. The eighteenth-century development of the Great Estates in London granted an interest in land, a building lease which provided a smaller business without much capital the opportunity to develop to the benefit of the landowner as custodian for their beneficiaries, the wider community and the small enterprising developer.

Developments are perhaps the last province of the independent entrepreneur: you hunt out opportunity, you dream up the project, you navigate through the regulatory maze, you seduce your funders, you enthuse your team and cover your eyes when writing the cheques, you make endless decisions on architecture, fittings, colours, textures, spaces, widths and furniture, you try and understand your customer, you present and promote the project the best way you can and hope that your sales are more than your costs.

This book is written from a developer's point of view. It is neither an apologia nor validation but a personal experience.

My Point of View

We read daily reports of rising house prices being fuelled by overseas investment while demand continues unabated. We all love our bricks and mortar. If we have any surplus cash from anywhere in the world, we would sooner have it invested in houses or apartments in London, New York and Paris than money left in the bank. Housing shares a role as part commodity and part investment. It has become a combination of a portfolio, savings, pension and the legacy we want to leave to our children. It doesn't function simply as a home. Maybe it never has?

Without sufficient new development keeping pace with demand, the price inflates. It follows the plain truth of supply and demand. Without reversing this condition, prices go on rising. The crisis in housing is in the supply. It is generally accepted that, were we able to increase our supply from the 100,000 homes we are currently building (in 2013 total new home completions were 109,660) up to 250,000 homes per annum, we might begin to see house price inflation align with wage inflation.[7]

What this book sets out to examine further is why that supply has traditionally lagged behind demand and how we might identify new ways to change this imbalance by creating more homes. I am promoting an independent movement in development, for developers that can make small projects interesting, attractive and loved by their neighbours.

We need to be more imaginative with how we manage our land supply in towns and cities so as to yield a better supply of new homes.

<u>Discovering more development opportunities within the city will accelerate building. I'd like to concentrate our attention towards the gap sites present in our urban fabric and find better ways of modifying the buildings that already exist so as to maximise their capacity.</u>

It is easy to let the status quo and the shortage of new homes continue. It allows volume housebuilders to continue to lobby for development on the Green Belt. They argue that parts of it are poor in quality and that the UK has, in percentage terms, more undeveloped countryside than other countries. They will suggest that ours would not suffer from more small-scale erosion. These big-scale interventions, homes numbered in hundreds and thousands, will always appeal to politicians. Garden City extensions have become a political expediency and a popular approach to more housing on Green Belt land.

I am not suggesting that this will stop. Volume housebuilders are like supermarkets; they are the giants and it's like asking them to stop selling branded food for the sake of the independents. When organic food was first mooted, it had not yet appeared on supermarket shelves but gradually, as organics grew to a movement, supermarkets had no choice but to supply them. I believe the same trend could influence what the volume housebuilders decide to offer.

We need to make a start with independent developments on gap sites. We need to educate the customer in how to demand of their developers both a dedication and passion towards experimenting with building in our cities. Only through that demonstration will new types of homes emerge. This should promote a fresh approach to development — one designed to enhance its surroundings. When we gaze over a bountiful garden we expect that new plants would add to its beauty. Gap site development by insertion should serve similarly to enhance its immediate surroundings.

History and the Current Condition

In the UK we have a long history of making housing for both rich and poor. We have examples of affordable housing with tithe cottages, workers homes in the Bournville tradition, homes for the underprivileged in the Peabody tradition, homes for churchmen and their families in the vicarage tradition and homes for the poor in the Parish tradition. We have examples of traditional private homes, the ubiquitous "Englishman's home is his castle", that is summed up by the combination of the detached, the semi-detached and the terraced housing typologies.

The dense urban fabric of Georgian and Victorian housing, now cherished, did sometimes result in homes that suffered overcrowding, became insanitary and finally slums. The Blitz and slum clearances made way for the big post-war public housing programmes. These estates occupy large parts of our landscape today. English towns and cities exemplify development for rich and poor alike — successfully integrated into the urban plan. The great pre- and post-war public housing schemes built, developed, owned and managed by the LCC (London County Council) and subsequently the GLC (Greater London Council), along with local authority housing across London, all demonstrate the heritage of housing for the disadvantaged built with a quality and passion by leading architects of their day.

The development of private housing was promoted politically following the First World War. Lloyd George when electioneering in Wolverhampton in November 1918 asked, "What is our task? To make Britain a fit country for heroes to live in."[8] This led to the election slogan, "Homes fit for Heroes". Nationwide we were building for a better future.

The land being developed was agricultural and followed the extensions of the suburban railway lines. "Metro Land" was sold by the railway companies. Developers were delighted to entice railway companies to new locations so that they could market their homes to commuters who could get to work easily. This, combined with the widening availability of long-term financing and mortgages, promoted the growth of suburban house types, providing a great boost to home ownership.

As a consequence, the rate of annual private house building in the UK rose from 125,000 in 1925 to peak in 1934 at just below 300,000.[9] Any developer or builder of new housing needs both the land and the permission to construct. In the 1930s this was straightforward. Plots were serviced by roads, railway stations were established and new homes were built to a standard specification and size to meet the demand and the price. In this golden age, the first Town and Country Planning Act of 1947 had not yet become law. This Act dictated that planning permission was required for development of land and therefore moved the power from the landowner to the state. In the five years from 1933 to 1937, an average of 62,000 private new homes were built each year in London.

Rather like the Great Estates, developed in the eighteenth and nineteenth centuries, quality reflected price. The Great Estates are urban areas of London that were developed by aristocratic families in the eighteenth and nineteenth centuries — I will refer to them throughout this book as examples of successful and cherished London developments. These areas include the Mayfair, Portman, Bedford and Grosvenor Estates. Rent was calculated per linear foot of frontage but fashion and location dictated the price. For example Bedford Square in Bloomsbury, which boasted facades set back from the pavement and generous front areas drove a premium, whilst Mare Street in Hackney, with its facades positioned on the pavement, did not.

By the twentieth century, houses were being sold freehold rather than rented on long leases with suburban house prices varying from £600 for basic to £1,200 for premium.[10] At the premium end, the desirable gentleman's residence was born, a label afforded to the detached houses with bigger frontages and wooden panelled hallways by the estate agents of the day. By reference to inflation tables, £600 then would be the equivalent of £30,000 today and £1,200 the equivalent of £60,000. This reinforces the point that sufficient supply will suppress inflationary pricing.

Such price differentiation continues today. Rightmove and Zoopla, popular internet sites for sales comparison, will report the value of each of our properties by reference to their size and postcode, with prices changing in line with fashions and taste. As a developer I am always looking for opportunities where value can be enhanced.

Fundamentally property development is the art of spotting where value could be exploited. I recall the discovery of those long forgotten large Victorian houses that had been changed from single family homes to multi-occupancy accommodation (bedsits). By the early 1970s, many of these houses became vacant and were suddenly development opportunities. As a young architect with an increasingly eager eye for property, I found a ready market for my services dividing these bigger houses into flats. For a flat fee of £300, I would sit down at my kitchen table and draw away into the small hours to provide my developer clients with sets of plans for such conversions.

The next opportunity was to convert Victorian warehouse buildings into spaces for loft-living. Developers realised that these cheap, redundant industrial buildings with open spaces, abundant light and attractive cast iron columns could be converted into studio and living spaces. I remember the thrill of finding these wonderful redundant factories that, at the time, could be bought at a price per square foot not much more than the equivalent cost of carpet. In a developer role I negotiated over the price of a former hat factory in a forgotten part of Smithfield with bored city agents to bring together a group of artists to make live-work studio spaces. Promoting the group to the planners and finding the contractor who could just about make the building habitable was a good lesson in developer skills.

As we began to recognise the development potential of these derelict buildings and we started to rescue them for new uses, we were welcomed by local authority planners. They recognised that the investment from a willing developer to bring these buildings back into use was beneficial. Today that trust between the developer and the local authority has disappeared.

Comparing the history of housing supply with car production, we observe contrary directions. In 1937, 390,000 cars were produced,[11] while a popular family car, the Austin 7 sold for around £150.[12] In 2014, the average cost of a similar family car was £15,000 and the UK's total production of cars was 1,500,000 units per annum.[13] Average house prices in London in the 1930s ranged from £600 - £1,000[14] and nearly 300,000 new private homes were built across the UK per annum (287,500 in 1934).[15] In 2014, the average house price across the UK was £180,000[16] and we produced just 100,000 units per annum.[17]

The analysis of car production in the years between 1937 and 2014 demonstrates the simple benefits of manufacturing efficiencies. While the 1937 Austin 7 remains an interesting car, it simply cannot be compared with its smarter, more energy efficient counterparts of today. Producing a limited number of handmade cars was a process shifted entirely through the invention of the production line. However with housing, we are still making handmade homes. Car production increased 500 times and despite the increase in sophistication, car price inflation has remained equal to movement in the Retail Price Index (RPI). On the other hand, house production has fallen three times while price inflation is over four times the RPI.

In the Chilean pavilion at the 2014 Venice Biennale there was a poignant display of a single signed, concrete prefabricated panel; the remnants of a system developed under the Soviet regime and manufactured in a special factory exported by the Soviets to President Salvador Allende in Chile.[18] This system constructed prefabricated housing across the communist states and their dependencies between 1945 and 1985. 170 million homes worldwide were constructed using the system. These, although considered archaic today, provided homes for

Shouldn't we all be developers?

approximately 500 million city dwellers that, in light of our current supply hiatus, is dramatic. Although dismissed and condemned, these efficiently manufactured developments managed to provide housing at the numbers that we need today.

London has always been a commercial city and has had a long history in the promotion of global free trade. Different governments throughout that history have benefited from taxing that trade. London's active participation in this has demonstrated its ability to be flexible, to change and develop to meet the demand and enterprise of its citizens. We face that same challenge today. We need to find ways to welcome, rather than resist, development at the centre of our cities as positive additions to our existing urban form.

Proposition

We have a crisis of supply in housing and we agree that we need more homes. London is part of a wider global market; it is predicted that 200,000 people every day will leave the countryside to start their new lives in the city.[19] London is not alone but will be a part of this population movement.

Such crisis is not new in the city's history; we have been here before. The Great Fire of London in 1666 destroyed 80 per cent of buildings, which required rebuilding in stone and brick. After 1863, with the opening of the first underground railway, the population of London grew from two million to six million people.[20] In 1945, after the war destroyed one in every six homes, London responded by constructing new public and private housing. At each of these moments in London's long history we have shown resilience, determination and invention in changing the city.

We have both the resource and culture and need to rekindle in London that spirit of enterprise to rise to our current housing challenge of 50,000 new homes per year. There are many different models of development and we need to encourage them all. Individual developers have the passion to make their own contribution. They do not find it easy to work precisely within overly prescriptive planning policies. Their enthusiasm and commitment should be encouraged.

London is a city of robust form. It is the city of choice for many from inside and outside the UK. Historically the city has benefited from new and intelligent development that evolves to meet the needs of its population. That is a tradition of change that needs to be endorsed. The word "crisis" presents opportunities for new ways of building and living. Land is fundamental to development and figures recently released suggest that 60 per cent of our redundant urban land is held by local authorities.[21] The disposal of this land by the public sector could contribute directly to the supply of these much needed homes.

I believe we can find sites and buildings to develop in the heart of our existing urban form. London has an area of approximately 1,500 square kilometres. This is a huge capacity and already an area of existing development.

We can learn to be better in the art of inserting new development into existing plots. Replacing lower density with more appropriate higher density. The open weave patterns of London grant us wonderful opportunities for a creative response to proliferation; working with our imagination to determine the appropriate development volume, delivering new buildings that make for positive additions to the city.

We have developers who can work at different scales and with different agendas. We have existing buildings with spaces surrounding them that have already been developed and feel full. Over the last 40 years, we have picked the low-hanging fruit. This next phase of housing for new generations is going to be both more complex and more interesting as a consequence.

In this book by Solidspace, we show examples of small insertions that seek to demonstrate 'Development as Art'. In Steen Eiler Rasmussen's history of London, he attributes the London house as Britain's great contribution to world architecture and adds this description:

> *The English House from this period is in accordance with the principles of Industrialism which in England was developing already in the eighteenth century. Each building is not an individual work of art, but a refined industrial product brought to perfection through constant selection during repeated serial construction. The virtues of this type of house are not to be sought in the expression of the elevation but in the brilliantly economical use of the narrow site.*[22]

I continue in my work to rediscover that historically simple way of making new homes. When I engage with a gap site, I build a complete picture in my mind of the form that could emerge. This form is three-dimensional, an enclosure bound by walls and roofs. It is sculpted to respect light to an adjacent window. Apertures are inserted into the walls and roofs to bring light and air to suit the internal plan.

My personal passion of experimentation with existing London housing is to take the stair as the centrepiece of this typical narrow, tall house and where in the eighteenth century it would "ascend in the middle of the house — is built up with beautiful marble steps and the whole construction is so delicate and slender that one can hardly believe one's own eyes."[23] I have embraced the pleasure of the stair and created spaces as extensions to half landings. In any dog-leg stair (a stair that doubles back on itself) these half landings are literally halfway up the full height of the floor. The use of this device became standard in most Victorian terraced houses in gaining access to the back extension at different levels. In dealing with the tight constraints of gap sites, I have extended the function of the stair to connect and create linked internal volumes.

This half level arrangement provides a sectional advantage to the lines of sight between one building and its neighbour. It is a helpful device to optimise space within the urban fabric. It makes new space that is attractive to the customer and adds value for the developer. It offers a more diverse and open-plan approach to our contemporary lives. Each project becoming individual, a site-specific building that, although following strict rules, emerges complete and designed especially for every site.

In all this endeavour I am fulfilling a single aspiration which is to exploit the volume, light and character of each of the gap site developments we undertake. I consider this to be the key attribute of contemporary space that is desirable and thus commands a premium. This is our reward for the work, care, time and consideration that goes into the independent developers' work in the city; then there is the passion that has no limit, just pleasure and pain in equal measure.

We have c
a perfect s

30 Shouldn't we all be developers?

Chapter 1: Planning

My Point of View

Our landscape of towns, cities and their buildings holds a special place in our hearts and minds — they are familiar. We recall with affection our childhood street and the bus stop where we would wait on our journey to school. The places we travelled to, the settings of our first romance are memories worth protecting. We watch with dismay as the familiarity of this landscape changes with the passage of modern life. This breeds in us all a resistance to change in our physical surroundings, one I feel has become more acute as change in other areas of our lives accelerates. We happily embrace change in the worlds of work, communication and the media. We depend upon our consumer durables; our intelligent mobile devices that deliver us data instantly and provide an ability to communicate with whoever, wherever and whenever we wish. We accept and welcome a changing digital world. We demand the latest technology.

Why then are we so resistant to changes in our own personal environment? It's not that we are unwilling to see physical change to our environment. On the contrary, it is of such concern, that we have constructed a complex system of planning responses to slow it down.

Current planning policy was not designed to meet our now overwhelming demand for housing. To generate an increase in supply, we need to densify the central areas of our cities to provide more building. Working at fine grain, block by block with the existing stock will inform these opportunities and will add to new sources of land for development. Infilling has its own validity but also comes with its own share of problems. The validity is that it is already part of the city, the street and the environment. Schools, shops, parks and transport all already at hand. It is attractive to the people who live and grew up there as well as the newcomers it invites. Its problem is that, as part of the city, it is in all our backyards.

Neighbours to new development as well as the local communities in which it sits are stakeholders by proxy and until they feel that the development is acceptable, they will continue to object. Gathering sentiment towards development from a more contemporary pool of social media could better reflect the concerns held by *all* those living in the surrounding area and not just the few that tend always to object. The view largely shared by active users of social media is that it gives them a voice where before they didn't have one. Social media's far wider reaching audience ensures that any negative feedback lodged against a developer will be taken more seriously so as not to harm reputation, therein providing better accountability to the local community stakeholders for whom the development is most likely to effect.

The attraction of newly found locations flagged as better suited to housing new development describes the economic vitality of London and how it remains active and attractive, thriving through a continuous process of its own reinvention. However, this process is in danger of becoming a victim of its own success.

The attraction of the rediscovered parts of our towns and cities follows a timeline. Traditionally the early adopters will pay the lowest entry price and as the success of the area grows, the price of the homes and other premises rises. Without therefore expanding supply, simply put, demand escalates price and new homes quickly grow unaffordable. Additional housing on gap sites can rebalance this dilemma in favour of customers.

Development should be of positive benefit to our communities and building with imagination and responsibility can serve to enhance and delight the conservation areas in which it exists or adjoins. The city's buildings are constructed over different centuries and built in varied shapes and styles. That difference enriches our experience provided it is constructed with a passion and an eye for beauty.

History and the Current Condition

What this tells us about planning is how deeply held in the English psyche the wider concerns of all neighbouring communities are to any development in their area. Maintenance of the status quo therefore becomes a more preferable endeavour than any support towards change. The system of planning has evolved to support this wider public concern with policies having developed to reinforce that status quo, whether geared towards conservation of landscape, buildings or parts of a neighbourhood — they have grown generically to rule over the planning decision making process.

Reviewing the origins of our current planning system, we can identify 1947 as the key date when the Town and Country Planning Act became legislation. Prior to that date the very notion of planning was more to do with matters of public health. Regulation of building starts after the Great Fire of London in 1666 with rules designed to avoid it happening again.[24] The Metropolitan Board of Works, established in 1855 (superseded by the London County Council in 1889) concentrated primarily, under the direction of Chief Engineer, Joseph Bazalgette, on responding to the Great Stink of 1858 and took responsibility for the construction of the sewers and supply of clean water to houses. It developed as a great civic institution, providing important communal services including roads, schools and public housing.

In the eighteenth century, the Great Estates had taken the lead in dictating the form of development over their urban land holdings. The 1947 Planning Act shifted the responsibility of determining the form and shape of development from landowner to state. The aristocratic landowners of the Great Estates expressed a feudal responsibility to both their tenants and their own land. They built, not only for themselves, but for their families' many future generations. This model proved so successful that all of these urban areas laid out in the eighteenth and nineteenth centuries still form the core of our conservation areas and listed buildings today.

It was a response to the growing urbanisation within our towns and cities that the basic human right of making a home for your family which, throughout civilisation has been undertaken without state involvement, moved from its simple beginnings to the heavily regulated, state controlled system of today.

In the period following the end of the First World War in 1918 — as soldiers were welcomed back as heroes — the pioneering Plotlands movement began. Plotlands were small pieces of land separated into regular plots designated for self build housing. Individuals were encouraged to build virtually anywhere to provide themselves with homes. There are charming incidences of old railway carriage and rolling stock reuse becoming romantic shacks and there remains an innocence and naïve beauty to these settlements in their rural locations. However, the public outcry over their lack of infrastructure (with resulting insanitary conditions) contributed to the ground swell response of planning control leading to legislation. Britain's age of free-wheeling development had disappeared. Building back-to-back housing was outlawed in 1909[25] and slum clearance legislation followed in The Housing Act of 1930.[26]

> In the current position, we have a plethora of planning legislation with national and local policies and guidelines so complex that we cannot now feel comfortable or positive about surrendering any part. On the contrary, we wish to add and impose even more control.

The situation has become the 'theatre of the absurd' where a threat of court action or judicial review leaves little flexibility in the hands of the local planners who administer the process. Much like prototyping in the product design world, building projects that genuinely strive for quality must follow an iterative process as teams improve their initial design through trial and investigation before moving it on to delivery.

The lack of trust in the system has forced planners to tightly draw their consents meaning that any design change made post-approval is in danger of becoming a breach of consent. One could reply, "Well, just don't make any changes", which although a perfectly valid response, determines a building be built to its earliest and least developed design iteration, allowing the quality of the finished development to suffer. A compromise usually passed on to its end users who must now live with it.

This assumes that planning is in control, but as Peter Wynne Rees claims in a recent *Financial Times* article, "the greatest thing about London is that it is unplannable. The worst thing about it is that it's unplanned".[27] Sporadic and spontaneous development in London has a long history. The reality of the situation is that developers promote, planners react and residents complain.

Building is proliferating in the city at all scales from the mega to the miniscule. The impact of a few new homes on a gap site is not the same as a new tower and mega development on a large site.

The reaction and restrictions imposed should be proportionate to the scale of development.

We agree that an abundance of new homes is needed to stand a chance of reversing unaffordable and unrestrained house price escalation for this generation and the next. Whilst holding a disproportionate expectation of financial tolls before we approve a development, we have created our perfect storm — a "combination of circumstances that aggravate a situation dramatically".

A planning system built upon a complex foundation of controls, overlaid with wider public mistrust of and distaste for development, wealthy overseas investors targeting homes as investment vehicles, an expanding population fuelling demand meeting ever strengthening regulation and a shortage of supply all provide the ingredients for that perfect storm.

Scanning opportunities for proliferation in central parts of our cities, we find that designated conservation areas are located exactly where we could benefit from more development. The planning system imposes a test and requires evidence to prove that new development will not be harmful to that conservation area. Invariably, in practice, this defaults back to the status quo or specific designation date of a conservation area hundreds of years after its development. This conservation ranks higher than any ongoing alteration, redevelopment or transformation of these buildings that seeks to bring them into contemporary use. It freezes these locations in time, condemning their future to a series of pale imitations of their past. It inadvertently encourages proposals that are lacking in character, colour and basic in shape and form as these have become the non-offensive, neutral attributes that prove the easiest pathways to gaining consent.

It is easy to make this sound ridiculous and supporters of conservation would answer that it is a necessary reaction to rapacious developers who would ruin our environment were such a system of control not in place. As a riposte I would ask that since all new development must have first passed these stringent sets of difficult tests, why then are the majority of the buildings that result so unsatisfactory?

Over-controlled development above ground has created some bizarre situations below. The shortage of housing, price rises and speculative value proposition has led to a rash of basement extensions below existing homes and gardens. The escalation of these types of development seem to be as a consequence of the relaxation of planning rules when applied to space below ground. It is an example of the way in which our wider fear of change to our environment can be bypassed when considering hidden subterranean extensions.

At the heart of this debate is the question of change. Clearly we don't want it, like it or condone it. This seems a particularly British position. If we look at Paris at the beginning of the 1980s, we discover the President Mitterand commissioned, IM Pei designed, glass pyramid providing a new entrance to the Louvre. It is located on an axis in the courtyard in one of the city's most important and historic public spaces — on a par with Trafalgar Square. This happened contemporaneously with the competition winning Ahrends Burton Korelek design proposal for an extension to London's National Gallery where, after much public heart-searching and the intervention of the Prince of Wales with his infamous carbuncle speech (1984), a disappointing wing by Robert Venturi and Denise Scott Brown was added. Meanwhile in Paris — a city dedicated to its history — the Louvre Pyramid seems to express the spirit of its citizens. This Grand Projet celebrates French culture with a potent contemporary piece of architecture. It is an example of the contrast between confidence and planning compromises in these two countries where the pyramid has emerged as the better building. There is a positive public acceptance of its iconography rather than the Sainsbury Wing extension at the National Gallery that has melted into the background.

Proposition

I believe that consistent and city-wide development on gap sites can yield new homes. These small sites, although disparate and patchy, run continuously throughout the city. Our challenge is to find ways of making these gap sites take supply and to encourage development here rather than have it forced out to the peripheries of the city. The gain is to our local economies, to our health, schooling and social services being agglomerated.

My proposition is not to change the process of planning radically, this has already been progressed, but rather rediscover the simple 'man with the oil can' approach of judicious easing of cogs in the machine that speeds supply. We can see that some simplification has already occurred; sites with less than 10 units are considered by most local authorities to be minor applications and have certain exemptions. Permitted development has been extended to include changes of use from office to residential, and finally building regulations allow and encourage a Type Approval where repetitive designs of houses only require a single consent.

With gap sites, development on each site is variable and particular. The different context is a guide to the right development envelope. A simpler rule-based approach could be applied to identify gap sites and set standard parameters for development massing. These rules already exist in planning policies; the impact of development on neighbouring property, daylight angles from adjacent properties, densities, design standards and heights of buildings relative to their street. New York planning codes provide examples of As-of-Right development, where the development volume and use are dictated but other aspects are left up to the developer.[28] The UK version would be different, (we do not operate quite within a grid city and we like our new buildings to proclaim their good neighbourliness) though tending towards it. Any rule-based system would give greater certainty to developers and promote better individual development quality. Developers would find a set of rules helpful, local authorities would benefit from easing their scarce resources and speeding up the process.

At present we have a system of planning that favours the big-scale intervention over the small-scale. These mega schemes connect volume housebuilders, with all their resources and professionals, with the local authority but leaves disappointment with both the local community and the consumers who desire a better and more bespoke offering. The result is far too much poorly designed housing, unsatisfied consumers and dull projects that do not create distinctive places.

The 'oil can man' approach seeks a simplified rule system to make the fine grain connection between a local community and a new breed of independent developer.

The shortage of supply is a challenge for London but learning from the past proves it has robustly adjusted and grown to accommodate its citizens. If we champion this smaller scale, independent developer, not only will they use their skills and imagination to build that supply, they will use their development instinct to identify these gap sites to deliver their projects. These imaginative and beautiful buildings could grow to a wider movement across the city and beyond, for Development as Art.

My Dream Scenario

I've seen a small site in Hackney in the auction. I check the local authority website and find it's been identified as a gap site. I load up the site data and print 1:200 scale plans. I rush off to view the site. I check the orientation of the sun and spend time figuring out its relationship with neighbouring buildings.

I like the street, its got patina. It's occupied by a derelict single-storey building and from the faded graphics, it looks as though it had been a bookmakers. On the other side of the street stands some 1960s public housing with its dominance of security shutters, a bus route and on the next corner, a nice pub. I spot a train on the elevated railway zipping past in the distance and across the road there's a convenience store, open all hours. A mature plane tree stands handsomely on the pavement. It all makes sense and gets me excited. I am feeling that first flush of passion as the site and I are beginning to make acquaintances. I walk the block searching for views into back gardens and mature trees, looking at door bells to see whether houses are subdivided, checking out bikes chained to railings, whether the colour of the front doors matches the Farrow and Ball paint chart and the long vista down the next road to the church at the end. At that minute the sun — now quite late in the day — makes its final appearance and lights up the gable wall of the next door house and there I see that important opportunity for evening drinks in the sunset.

I decide on the location of the entrance, that moment of truth where I remind myself of some long forgotten

Architectural Association jury of my youth where a tutor's single question was always the same, "You come in where?" That question has stayed with me forever and I now pose it to myself on every development site I spot. Playing with the plan, dancing it around the section and around the Type Approval volume, now gives me the design opportunity I crave. It shifts, I sketch and I am beginning to see a way. I add a section and realize that it gives me a bit more space with a half level dig down, a few more strokes of the pen reveal the plan and section fixed. With the plan settled, I calculate the floor area to get to the size, run the appraisal and get to a price for the auction. A check of the legals and I'm there and bidding. This time success and I wonder as I walk away — reeling from the euphoria of the winning bid — just how long it will be before we can finish and sell.

Land is to developme what the [...] is to the a[...]

Shouldn't we all be developers?

Chapter 2: Land

My Point of View

To make a meal you need ingredients. To make development that ingredient is either land or an existing building. Land is to development what the canvas is to the artist. It is the starting point. The home is what the developer offers the customer.

The developer must construct their dream, their vision, on a site that is rooted to one place. It cannot move, but over time it can be changed. The projects need to work on the site. We may all dream of sites on leafy roads with big gardens but the inescapable reality is one of adjoining railways, main roads and small gardens. Development on gap sites challenges the imagination of the developers to overcome those negatives through their design approach. Every site is capable of redevelopment. Each of these transformations triggers an elaborate, expensive and complex process.

The volume housebuilders claim that inner-city land is scarce, that their preferred option for expanding supply is to build on the Green Belt. To redesignate farmland to building land will always be an attractive proposition, it has a self-serving simplicity. We believe that we have choices. London has plenty of development opportunity but it must first be teased out, viewed with a new lens to identify gap sites.

It might be obvious but worth recording that all development activity begins with land ownership. Ownership brings control over the site. That control extends to selling, leasing and developing. Traditionally, landowners did not develop themselves, they facilitated others to do so on their land.

Today, global capitalism is enmeshed in London, we should remember that whilst the physical land is immovable, all ownership rights are transferable to anyone, anywhere on the globe.

The land may be in London, the ownership in the Caribbean, the owner's residence in Hong Kong and the sale made to a new owner in New York, without any of the parties ever having met. The home in question remains in London and its value is fixed to the London market.

As capital gains tax from property until April 2015 was exempt if ownership remained offshore, this goes some way towards understanding why investing in London has been such an attractive proposition to non-UK residents.[29]

Real estate prices are fixed by London's supply and demand constraints. A global market brings with it price volatility and makes for a fast and speculative market.

It is of no surprise therefore that a trading market exists for parcels of land at all stages of pre-development, even though the site's saleability disappears as soon as construction begins. This helps to explain a conundrum in land supply; holding land back from construction allows it to be traded and its value to go on growing.

When Government releases statistics showing the pipeline of sites with consents, one might ask why these consented sites do not provide more homes?[30] With the cost and effort of obtaining consents for development and the market reality that land is tradable before starting construction, it is therefore tempting for investors to take their profit and trade their sites. This frustrates housing supply, pushing it onto the next owner and the future. Land trading is often serial, with the same piece traded many times. The current system of public sector land supply needs to be overhauled to stop land trading and to use these parcels directly for the building of new homes.

It is easy, when bombarded by articles reporting house price inflation, astronomical land prices and forbidding restrictions on development all going hand in hand to fuel demand and starve supply, to feel the problem is intractable. In looking at small scale gap sites and how we can encourage them to take more supply, can we borrow the invention of air rights which, although firmly established in New York and other American cities, is not yet established in the UK?

We have recently established the relationship between development and infrastructure and are seeking to tax it with our new CIL (Community Infrastructure Levy) charges. We are used to a long and inventive relationship between fixed, real property to its location and different transferable rights that move anywhere. Transferable air rights as a further invention of this raw material might just confound that Mark Twain maxim, "buy land, they're not making it any more", with a whole new set of possibilities.

History and the Current Condition

I start the story with the Domesday Book of 1086 that identified the ownership and value of each parcel of land in England at that date. This first inventory of land and its owners has been the basis of subsequent land law. It has since been the English tradition for these original land parcels to be divided again and again. I refer to this origin in history, as I believe it to be at the root of understanding some of the more peculiar nature of English land law. This has been governed by what we refer to as common law; traditions evolving over centuries, case by case, as disputes become resolved. From this common law root, the legislation follows. Rights in common were needed for access and became the precursor to roads, rights of way and other rights required for development.

When the Great Estates decided to exploit their land holdings in Belgravia and Westminster, they sought a method for purchasers of long leases to invest in their land holdings to construct houses on them. Firstly, they took the initiative to lay out the streets, the garden squares and the design of the houses and townscape, but passed the costs of construction on to the leaseholders. They controlled the design and the specification, requiring that their developers use their bricks, paint houses in their approved colours and make every piece of ironwork uniform. Today we appreciate the heritage that this particularly British vision of the house and square has left to us.

The particular nature of the legal agreement is a lesser known or understood element of that heritage; the combination of long lease and occupational tenancy that made their very development possible. These legal structures offer important lessons for today.

The deployment of patient capital can and must be a force for good in the creation of resilient new urban neighbourhoods. Historically, building houses to sell was not the kind of investment that institutions wanted. It is higher risk, shorter term and it is difficult to capture the long-term capital growth or to justify the required investment in placemaking. The estate model allows for long-term value growth, scalable capital exposure and is a model for holistic investment in places, not just buildings. The long investment horizon allows design, stewardship and management principles to be applied over time. This permits management of the physical environment through periods of change and supports the development of the community from creation to maturity. This leads to a long-term investment capable of delivering income and capital growth to investors, and providing a high quality environment

> *for occupiers. Not only has the estate model been a great investment model for landlords, it has been— and can continue to be—good for London, creating carefully managed neighbourhoods that are among the greatest places in any city.*[31]

Building consent gives land added value. That value is made up of a combination of different elements: the development volume and the number of units. With urban sites, there are numerous development risks: restrictive covenants in favour of neighbouring land holders or infrastructure providers such as Network Rail, land pollution from previous uses of the site as industrial or process-based use, taking into account the claims for rights to light for adjoining development that could limit the proposed development and modified access to meet standards that may also require small parts of adjacent land to be purchased.[32]

I recall a small development on a backland site, previously used as a furniture factory, where I wanted to build housing. There was a small lane leading to the site, one that seemed just about useable provided a lorry driver reverse into it. All seemed fine until a discussion with the fire brigade reminded me, when arriving at a fire, they were not prepared to reverse their fire engines in to deal with an emergency. I assured the Fire Chief that it wouldn't be a problem but he was unconvinced and suggested we try it out on site. The day arrived, the fire truck turned up, went into position, made the turn and promptly came to a stop against a brick pillar on my neighbour's land. It was clear my bravado had failed and that, sometime later, (and substantially poorer), my neighbour agreed to sell me a small triangular slip of their land, I survived the fire crews' mirth, negotiated this necessary easement and the development was built.

Local Authorities are the owners of numerous historically acquired sites. Recent reports have suggested that Local Authorities own up to 60 per cent of the potential undeveloped land in London.[33] The old property industry adage "all sales are only triggered by death or divorce" is very pertinent now in the case of public land, where the trigger is the need for cash. A cash-strapped local authority will look for redundant sites that they can sell to plug gaps in their budget.

Local authority land sales are either by auction or by public tender. In all these cases, sites are sold to the highest bidder. This method of disposal means that the public sector seller can simply satisfy themselves that they have, at the time of sale achieved best value.[34] It is clearly simpler then to dispose of a site by public auction or public tender and report to members or audit committees that market exposure and market price achieved were the best possible at the time of sale. However, when examined in retrospect, the sites are often seen as having not obtained quite the result first predicted. When the purchase results in a trade, the productive use of the land to make new homes is delayed and made more expensive.

This is often known by the title of a children's game, "pass the parcel". This prompts a change of price, mostly upwards, but sometimes downwards.

Each time the land parcel is traded, profits are taken. This generates a price escalation and puts pressure on the planners to increase the amount of development. The land profit goes into the pocket of the trader. The local authority doesn't benefit and the supply of homes is delayed. The sale has gone from best to worst value and the use of the land for more housing supply has not been achieved.

I favour the legal agreement used by the Great Estates, where the freeholder continued to own and the leaseholder completed the development. This arrangement of long lease sales, whilst retaining the freehold, remains simple, transparent and grants sufficient legal authority to make it a stable and understood system of land disposal.

It is clearly in the public's interest to make sure that land in their ownership needs to be directed towards the production of more homes. Partnering arrangements that disallow trading but encourage development-led house building should be supported.

Proposition

In this chapter on land supply, we've seen how land traders have dominated public sector land supply without delivering development. It would be nice to think that they could be persuaded to contribute to supply. It could be argued that they do by finding the site, gaining consent and selling it on to the final developer, but the cost of the arbitrage and the delay in the time it takes to bring it into productive use has to be another cog in the machine that the 'oil can man' needs to examine. The alteration to the publicly owned land disposal process was addressed by the 2015 budget statement. The Chancellor announced, "Establishing a London Land Commission to identify public sector land for development, helping London to ensure development on all of its brownfield land by 2025."[35]

While this is welcome, I would like to suggest widening its terms of reference to include gap sites which should be disposed of to smaller independent developers in a different way.

The London Land Commission (LLC) should assemble these parcels solely to promote the development of new homes. The LLC would not be the developers, but would enter into commercial arrangements with these independent developers to construct new housing on their land. The receipts from the completed homes would be held by the LLC to resource more disposals plus any surplus arising being used by the Greater London Authority to fund new public housing. The role of the agency would be to optimise the value of their land parcels for this wider benefit of London housing.

Whilst not all gap sites are publicly owned, reasonable proportions are.[36] The public sector would be best served by ensuring that any land disposal was directly connected with the provision of land for new homes.

Often, in the past, when Local Authorities wished to dispose of land for custom build or design-led development, the pressure of demand in the market place, driven by the profitability of land trading, frustrated this intention and forced the hand of the well-intentioned local authority by placing the land in the auction market and taking the cash receipt. The proposed LLC would immediately intervene and avoid that happening. The LLC should be vested with all local authority redundant land parcels.

The LLC, having collected these redundant buildings and land parcels in a single bank, would employ its own expertise to offer these sites out to a development marketplace that may only purchase to develop rather than to trade on the land. The LLC would transfer the land, subject to building agreements, where the developer pays the land receipt at the point of sale of the completed home. The LLC would then receive a percentage of that sale price. The New Town Corporations operated in similar ways providing surpluses back to the Treasury.

The function of the LLC has been stated to help London meet its target of 400,000 new homes. This would be much improved were it to encourage and promote the development of small, fractured sites that occur throughout local authority land holdings. It is a centralised collection point and ownership agency. Its powers are limited to disposal on building agreements thereby ending land trading at a stroke.

My Dream Scenario

It has become my regular habit to tap into the LLC's website early on Wednesday mornings when the latest bank of sites has been announced. I scan the normal length of listings of about 20 different sites. I am registered in category 3: sites from 0.1-0.3 hectares with development capacity of up to 10 units. The LLC has a number of bands from 1 to 5 reflecting the different sizes and capability of the range of developers who regularly use the service.

I return to gaze at the screen where one of my favourite types of site catches my eye — 0.1 hectares next to a railway, a redundant old caretaker's house. The site is long, narrow and tapering. It's in Islington's fringes, an area I like and one where I have made successful developments in the past. I download the tender pack. We now regularly call our team meetings for Thursday afternoons and I clear my diary to make sure that I can visit the site in the morning.

At our team meeting I show the photos and the downloaded packs and we agree which site to go for. The bid documentation is quite weighty and we have decided that we need to be selective and only go for one or maximum two in any given week.

The submission has to be accompanied by pre-qualification statements that confirm that we will enter into the LLC's standard building agreement, to build in accordance with their guidelines, and third party proof of funds. We are able to use the same pre-qualification statements each time we bid.

We decide which of the sites to bid for and begin the process. We decide on the level of the bid and the outline design at the final meeting before the deadline. The LLC are very good at dealing with the bids. They operate a shortlisting usually of the best three. For the last stages there are interviews with the members of this shortlist. The interview panel includes an architect, a surveyor and a lawyer who rotate and serve on the LLC, providing their combined experience to help the selection. These interviews and questioning from the expert panel are often helpful.

So far, we usually get awarded the sites around 50 per cent of the time. This is perfect for us as a small-scale developer, leaving us with about eight sites a year that we are working through with 30-50 units being developed. When the scheme was first mooted, many of the larger housebuilders suggested that it would not work and was too small. Intriguingly, the level of interest has been phenomenal, from small developers as well as the growing band of custom builders who participate. The LLC recently announced that the initiative had reached 25,000 new home starts two years since its launch and that they predicted annual delivery on their sites to increase to 30,000 over the next five years.

What has astonished City Hall is just how many gap sites had emerged from the detailed analysis of redundant public sector land. The LLC had been able to harness a completely new and enthusiastic set of developers and community structured custom builders who had brought forward a wide variety of development proposals. This prompted the press to cite this enormously popular and competitive movement as Development as Art.

The devel[oper,]
the restau[rant,]
and the a[rtist,]
his chef

56 Shouldn't we all be developers?

Chapter 3: Design

per as
ateur
chitect

My Point of View

Good design is enduring but infinitely rewarding. It operates at different levels in our lives; from emotional responses to colours — warm reds and cool blues — to the tactile enjoyment of materials and textures. We'll deliberate over rough wood versus smooth marble, right through to the ingenuity of how our interior space works with the intelligent functionality of a kitchen and the pleasure of the spacious volume of a sitting room. When extended to the exterior of our homes, we enjoy the simplicity of a brick, its colour and texture, the proportion of windows belonging to a facade and the punctuation of a dormer or gable to a roof line. Design is fuelled by choice whether over homes, cars, clothes, furniture, phones, watches or cameras. These choices are made so much more enjoyable when drawn from across many influences and examples.

Gap sites intrigue me — each one offering something entirely different to the last. They stimulate design innovation and variety. Gap sites are poignant. They are part of the history of the city. They connect adjacent buildings and spaces. They are leftover places where development can proliferate. I imagine the form that could fill this void and how the internal spaces can be arranged. I see a site for sale and in my endless wandering of the city, I pursue the prey, turn my eye up and down the street and relish the beginnings of a relationship with a plot. Rooted to the spot, my imagination is sparked and I start by measuring the opportunity. I pace around and start recording the site's boundaries and the flank walls to the back and to the front. I trace the sun's path, I register the trees, the views and the gaps. I imagine what might be built. How high could the building rise? What obstacle, stray window, odd pipe or random flue would block the path to redevelopment? What are the constraints of the adjoining buildings? What is the character of the neighbourhood?

The word 'context' as part of UK planning policy is one loved almost to the point of worship. Context is the relationship between old and new. Whether that question refers to the end-use, shape, height or materials, it is always a judgment call as to whether the proposed fits with the existing. This test is entirely subjective, often misunderstood and commonly defaults to promoting imitation rather than originality. Inserting a new building into context is the opportunity for an intelligent and creative response from its designer. It can be answered by blending or contrasting with its surroundings. Both are valid design responses.

Design excellence is driven by individual developers as clients who want to create legacies of good domestic architecture. The aim for me is always a new vernacular, not slavish imitation, but homes made to emerge from their particular location. I want to make buildings that stand as positive additions, using materials and shapes that are part of the neighbourhood vocabulary.

I think of its equivalence in cooking where ingredients and dishes are locally sourced. It is a slow but engaging process. Unlike the housebuilders of the 1930s, whose regimented schemes marched along arterial roads in step, a veritable semi-detached procession; ours is a process of surgery — weaving and modelling shape and form to sit comfortably within its context.

History and the Current Condition

Looking at domestic architecture in the UK, we're able to chart a history of styles rich in their variety. The architecture of the simple, domestic home has been traditionally driven by builder and developer. Urban housing in the UK dating back to medieval times has followed plot divisions based on a grid of party walls. Steen Eiler Rasmussen in his definitive book on London states:

> *The common little house of which there have been built thousands and thousands is only sixteen foot broad (5.00m). It has probably been the ordinary size of a site since the Middle Ages.*[37]

This is a trend reinforced by the rebuilding of the city after the Great Fire of London and continues with the terraced and semi-detached housing that covered our streets and neighbourhoods from the eighteenth century right through to the twentieth century. The terraced house is a British invention that offers a consistent and familiar backdrop to our streets. What I find intriguing as a model of urban development is the ease with which the terraced house fits so comfortably into its different site conditions, whether on streets that run up hills, turn corners, plots with narrow and wide fronts, funny-angled sites, land next to railways, land next to parks and two to five storeys, it has such ubiquity that it manages to fit in everywhere. I realise that our beloved terraced house in all its forms is a brand; it is desired, it is cherished, it is instantly recognisable, loved and above all, it compounds Steen Eiler Rasmussen's sentiment that "London's contribution to architecture is simplicity."[38] London is famously unplanned and has grown in a haphazard fashion. It began with independent villages connected by lanes and ended as an amalgamation infilled with development everywhere. Those lanes turned to roads, the roads to streets and as such, the city took shape. Terraced houses were extended at the front as well as the back, entering the commercial life of the city as well as the domestic.

If we look hard, we can see waves of development like the patterns of tree rings, layering out from these village hubs to join together in a continuous urban form.

As these hubs grew, they began to accommodate the different building types that allowed the modern city to function. Its urban distinction steadily acquired where moments of change would occur: a corner, a crossing of two streets or an interchange, all posing as intriguing anomalies in the urban form, creating the openings that now make up the bulk of our informal public spaces. Unlike the great public spaces of European cities, ours are wonderfully casual by comparison.

Charting the history of London's development draws our attention towards growth spurts that define aspects of its distinguishable style. Innovative answers to the call for housing can be found with social housing in Alexander Road, Camden, built by Neave Brown in 1969 — at first hated and unfashionable, now loved and listed — exemplifying development designed and conceived with its own aesthetic. Other twentieth-century social housing examples include: in east London, Denys Lasdun's Keeling House, Erno Goldfinger's Balfron Tower and in west London, Goldfinger's Trellick Tower. These all demonstrate a history of social housing built with the moral purpose of housing London's needy. As a part of London's wider housing stock, they sit comfortably alongside the Peabody buildings and the Mansion blocks that have found their way into the London amalgam of styles. These examples serve to reinforce how robust the

London urban context is and most importantly, how capable it is of reinvention, provided it has its own independent design integrity.

The desire for a terraced house in an urban context is similar to the wish for the country cottage with roses round the door. It is an idealised aspiration. The conventional design of bedrooms upstairs and living rooms downstairs holds a strong cultural attraction, encapsulating what the English desire most; their own home complete with staircase.

This I believe makes up the DNA of the spaces we call home. When facing the challenge of redevelopment, we must look for a design approach that discovers new forms of generic building that work as well as the terraced house and that can sit on each and every gap site available.

Restaurants in cities all over the world have managed to remain independent by offering their customers variety, care with their ingredients, the imagination of the chefs, table service and the overall decor all serving as attractive pulls. A healthy design aesthetic for gap sites is comparable to our cherished independent restaurants. The developer as the restaurateur and the architect his chef. They can make buildings that whilst contemporary, acknowledge and build upon historic architectural traditions. Let's exercise our right to demand good intelligent design in place of overblown developments cloaked in facades of indistinguishable ersatz architecture. In this age of social media we have better access than ever before to the wider held community view. We are all familiar with serving the customer. Independent developers care about their customers and can encourage them to use the internet as a communication channel for their responses.

Propositions

In many instances, gap sites are relatively small and as such, offer good breeding ground for design originality with the insertion of new buildings.

For design to succeed it needs to be iterative, following a path of minor but important shifts as it journeys from conception to realisation.

The creative process starts with a wider vision, maturing with every drawing and design iteration, pared or embellished to give its best performance on opening night when all is revealed.

We want to encourage the intelligent and considered redevelopment of gap sites. Independent developers invested in these principles should be trusted with their architects, to make something wonderful that enlivens the neighbourhood and establishes a new vernacular for our next surge of development. Our 'oil can man' should be encouraged to ease the bureaucratic burden.

To enhance supply of homes we need to densify these gap sites and encourage, rather than stunt, their growth.

A critique of this analogy is in the difference between the fleeting memory of a restaurant meal and the permanent mark of development. Cedric Price, the radical architectural thinker considered these matters. He was a life-long member of the professional body of the demolition industry and maintained that all buildings should be thought of as having a beginning, a middle and an end — the end being demolition. London's great strength has been its ability to constantly remake itself in order to meet new and relevant economic drivers. The need for the replenishment of new housing is exactly that. Roman, Medieval and Tudor London have all virtually disappeared in this process of demolition and renewal.

We should grant the architect/developer teams more clarity with simpler sets of planning rules. George Ferguson, past president of the RIBA and current mayor of Bristol, introduced the concept of x-listing which would permit the demolition of buildings that had become 'cankers' in their neighbourhood.

I support this and suggest that if a development, after 30 years, remains so offensive, overpowering or seriously damaging to the environment, the community can request of the authority to use its powers to seek demolition. This mechanism is parallel to the process of listing and that 30 years would need to pass from construction for this sanction to become effective. That is the period for a new building to be confirmed for listing and therefore, by fairness, this should be the same period for a building to be listed for demolition.[39]

When a building is listed, the architecture has been deemed to be of such cultural significance that it merits statutory protection. This process is established in law. The listing regime imposes the decision and the responsibility on the owner at the time. The owner is passive in the process but subject to the notification. As this 30 year rule is a good period for buildings that delight, the same timescale can be used for buildings that offend. This is an ultimate sanction. Demolition is a draconian power and would clearly help focus the mind of the community, developer and architect to ensure that they build to delight rather than to offend.

My Dream Scenario

After my visit to the site and the success of our bid to the LLC, we have secured a small site in Islington. I decide to collaborate with a new, promising young architect called Arnaud whose work I admire. It's always a challenge briefing these architects. They come in different flavours from flat, disconnected and enigmatic to overly helpful and enthusiastic about the project. I enjoy either as long as they have the talent to deliver that special design.

As developer, I establish the brief and with the Solidspace brand as our marketing label, it is important that these principles are clearly conveyed to the architect before they proceed. We prepare our initial design as part of our bidding process, fixing some of the key parameters of the project. We work together. Collaborative working of course presents its benefits and its drawbacks. It requires a sharing of ideas which some designers can find hard to accept. When they do however it proves the most rewarding part of the creative process, adding to its depth and the pleasure in its making. Gap sites are really a joy, they belong to their own genre. Armed with the brief, the words of encouragement, the site visit and the orientation, the architect disappears to further explore and carve out that design.

They return with their set of sketches. I prefer hand drawings, models, photomontage or anything that conjures a good feel for the site proposals. We debate the architecture; where the light will fall, the expression of the wall and the connection with the site. We learn quickly that, for the architect, there are three keys to their design: that faded industrial door with its many peeling layers of paint on the old warehouse opposite, the handsome, mature horse chestnut that lies at the end of the site and a series of battered old garden walls that surround the site — standing up more by habit than any kind of structural integrity. We learn that Arnaud believes that the materiality, the light and the window apertures need to strike a chord with these elements. The entire design becomes an enticing play of threes.

We debate. We sketch. Something's cooking, we begin to smell and even taste it. We settle on the idea and proposal, both pleased it has come back just as we imagined. We ask our quantity surveyor to run the costs. We blanch at the result. He reminds us using that *well worn refrain that, "It is always more for anything unusual". We invite the engineer to define the structure and in-situ concrete wins out. Arnaud wants to respect this backland site with a rainscreen of low level concrete, black painted corrugated iron, big hefty timber windows and heavy doors. I love it. It's distinctive and sits well as both a geometric and finished volume in this forgotten corner of Islington.*

This distinctive scheme needs some selling, not only to our own customers but to the wider community that it will sit alongside. As developers, we are pledged to the engagement of this wider community. We work hard at developing the narrative, prompting the engagement of the wider public in the hows and whys of the site proposals. Our online forum engages in debate and feedback. All is open and accessible in the public domain and since the Type Approval has already been obtained it becomes a pleasurable engagement with the wider public.

We commence building and inevitably it goes over time and budget but benefits from a universally positive reception. It sells well to our customers and wins many awards for Arnaud, whose reputation is growing. Design, creativity and example have been blended to show how imaginative this development can become and we as developers enjoy the success of another completed piece of Development as Art.

What if J[o
made hom[

Chapter 4: Brand

My Point of View

The long-term shortage in housing supply has allowed housebuilders to distance themselves from their customers. This is in stark contrast to examples of successful brands where customers are respected, understood and praised constantly for their attention and support. These brand success stories use every channel available to make and maintain that connection, deploying highly skilled methods of communication to seduce customers into a family-like circle of faith.

A key component to the success of these brands is their valuation of trust. Once a reputation of trust is established and a brand wins its following, long-term value is achieved with continuing stakeholder buy-in or desire. These are the foundations upon which they build customer aspiration to engage with their brand and its products or services. The customers cross a line, becoming brand ambassadors. They have extended their desirability to loyalty. Successful brands need to be loved.

When brands choose to pitch their values they need to be genuine. They must be values shared by company and customer alike. The internet — serving as the all-seeing watchdog — will quickly reveal to customers and competitors whether a brand's values are disingenuous. Loyalty to successful brands grows so strong it can be mistaken for some sort of religious devotion. This connection between a brand and its supporters has a depth and a strength. It works in two directions, making a brand accountable to its end users. It is vital the customer believes the brand's values reflect their own. By definition, a super-brand is able to use the power of their brand to build on their consumer popularity and expand their market. These super-brands have demonstrated how to disrupt the status quo and emerge as the dominant players in their fields.

An emergence of housing brands equally invested in these principles could have a surprisingly beneficial effect on the way in which the public view development. This two-way communication centred on trust and commitment from the customer and accountability from the manufacturer could re-empower consumers, extending to them the right to demand a quality from their suppliers not currently present in the market. To illustrate this further, I would ask the rhetorical question: What if John Lewis made homes? John Lewis is a trusted brand with a cache understood by many. Followers would positively welcome John Lewis branded housing next door to them for they would trust the brand to act in as considerate and thoughtful a manner possible so as not to disrupt their lives or run an untidy site during construction. They would expect the brand to deliver on their promise of quality, carefully priced housing, good value and customer service as principles upheld throughout.

Volume housebuilders state that they are brands. They certainly have a product range, provide large-scale supply and are responsible builders, but in my mind their product is not of the quality to cultivate adherence, love or the loyalty of their customers as can be found elsewhere with examples of brands successfully adopted by large sections of the public.

As we see the results of survey after survey, we learn that 75 per cent of those asked would not even consider buying a new home.[40] We find ourselves closer to the bottom of a food chain in a housing market where our volume housebuilders prefer buy-to-let investors, whether from the UK or abroad, to genuine homeowners. Homeowners have closed the door on these housebuilders opting instead for period properties (of which there are only so many to go around) over anything contemporary or really even urban. This nostalgic return to the past for me speaks to a deeper failure on the part of the producer in providing attractive alternatives for consumers to believe in.

From a branding point of view, we could not be more dysfunctional. With little or no trust left, no heroes in housing worth believing in and an alarming absence of desirable housing products, we are in the midst of a wonderful market opportunity for a new breed of independent producer to emerge, working to disrupt this clearly arcane condition.

The setting of new precedents through design innovation could elevate us to a fresh understanding of what our homes should be.

Independent developers working on gap site development in their locality, who maintain a strong presence on the ground and who build new homes carrying identity and originality, firing the imagination of their customers, could stand to profit in a market rife with consumer disenchantment.

Consider a new, collective housing brand made up of independent producers similar to the groups of coffee shops, artisan bakeries and organic butchers that have benefited from such surge in popularity, often clustered together in the minds of consumers. The suppliers may be diverse or loosely connected, but collectively they make up a community of brands whose principles are aligned. These have grown to movements where individual commitment and excellence as a personal crusade have met with the strengthening consumer response to fight back against the big, faceless corporate brands. Customers do need to be able to trust the integrity of their suppliers.

History and the Current Condition

When searching for new homes we conjure up names of familiar volume housebuilders such as Persimmon, Crest, Taylor Wimpey, Barratts and Berkeley Homes. These are names we may recognise; however, they aren't like the brands we find in food, clothes or cars. With these other consumer products, we often share a culture with the brand. They have worked hard to build our allegiance. We defend our commitment to these brands. We have become members of their club. Customer loyalty is what all brands need.

I use this to introduce the marketing language used by the volume housebuilders. They boast of luxury and suggest a lifestyle. They imply that living in their developments will miraculously transform you, the purchaser, into the luxurious lifestyle photos they show. The reality is that the best their brand stands for is overseas sales, off-plan, with products designed for rental occupation.[41] Their purchasers make their investment in the Central London residential market where they will receive income from renters and hope for speculative gain amounting from a growth in value. This is a business model driven by high demand for new homes in London and a scarcity of supply.

The volume housebuilders focus their efforts on building their land supply.[42] They limit their exposure, employing design firms that understand their product and that can get them their planning consents. They use small-scale contractors and maintain traditional contracting, whereby the client invites bids for the construction work, to use their not inconsiderable buying power to get the lowest price. They use their powerful lobbying with government to persuade planning to accept that their developments look and feel as identical as they can. This is an efficient model — it takes land and recycles it into effective new housing for an investment market. As a consequence of this activity, London has grown its base of the private rental sector (PRS) by sales to overseas landlords.[43] Neither these producers nor their products have a brand that engages or entertains a public that love them. Volume housebuilders are not and never will be an Innocent or an Apple. They pride themselves on professionalism and service, promising to deal with repairs quickly and promptly. Their's is a business model that meets the ambitions of their shareholders and that of myriad investors. They operate at a scale of delivery that has become close to monopoly.[44] They make public pronouncements whilst lobbying Government to release Green Belt land upon which they may grow their businesses and supply more to their overseas investment customers.

Volume housebuilders would contest this argument. They would agree that their inner-city or central city apartment blocks are predominantly owned by overseas investors. The percentage in Central London locations is up to 85 per cent of sales but out of town, where the product range is predominantly one of houses with some apartments, their sales are primarily to owner occupiers.[45]

The business model reality that volume housebuilders improve their profitability by constraining supply — which acts as a brake on the construction of new homes — is a promise missing from their marketing brochures.

The volume housebuilders are not offering products of distinction, rather relying upon the scarcity of housing generally and their reputation for reliability.

The priority for the volume housebuilder is land rather than the home itself. They have fostered powerful partnerships with Government, delivering wider regeneration initiatives on big-scale brownfield sites. These outcomes, whilst important in their own right, have had little to do with product or brand.

Each of the cogs powering the mechanics of development is engaged in a triangle of power where volume housebuilders, alongside Central Government, are on top, and the poor customer and the local community are forever squashed beneath their weight. Introducing brand as a new cog in this machine represents an opportunity to upturn this triangle, re-empowering customers, independent providers and the local community so that they may work harmoniously on small and local developments rather than rely on the provision of new homes to be supplied from this top down status quo. The principle remains clear; a brand can build trust between itself and the public. This gives an opportunity for a new collective of independent producers to make housing that can win the hearts and minds of a new generation of buyers.

Proposition

When a company extends their range of products into a brand, their corporate ethos needs to follow. Subsequently their activity, behaviour and organisation, including their product range, must reflect their brand values. The housing they produce needs to have a design that is identifiable. It needs personality and character that is recognisable, appreciated and loved by its customers.

I would cite Poundbury, the development undertaken by the Prince of Wales with architect, Leon Krier in Dorchester, Dorset, as an obvious example of a housing brand. It attracts its supporters and its critics. It spawns look-alikes in other parts of the country that carry signs of its nostalgic look and feel, but seldom of its quality. It has familiarity, created through its hotchpotch of an architectural history book with iconography collected from around the globe but placed in Poundbury. It has a well thought out layout and landscape of streets, pathways, surfaces, planting, lights and railings. The public like it and other communities in other parts of the country recognise and support it. I am not advocating or arguing for more Poundburys, rather demonstrating what a brand in housing can look and feel like.

Brands need access and availability. Once a brand achieves desirability, the public want to engage with it, buy, own and to cherish it. The brand holder cannot afford then to put their reputation or their brand at risk. As custodians of the brand, they have implicitly entered into a relationship with the wider public that includes local residents. The brand, therefore, brings with it social responsibility.

This wider collective of independent producers becomes attractive to the places where they develop because the brand they offer is variable, is distinctive, relates to its location and reflects the community held beliefs. This could make development an undertaking welcomed and positively supported, softening the local tendency towards resistance.

What healthy competition and brand awareness has done for foreign housing markets is to drive up quality and drive down price, whilst maintaining accountability to customers. The Japanese build 1.2 million new homes a year.[46] Their housing market features Toyota and other named consumer brands invested in the business of making new homes. Muji sell their own branded homes in Japan, available in-store. Those houses and their occupants are participating in Muji's shared brand ethos. In the UK, where housing brands are less prevalent, there is an emerging trend as certain independent developers move towards this branded concept: notably so with Urban Splash, Manhattan Loft, YOO, Pocket Living, WikiHouse and our own Solidspace.

I believe that independent producers building homes in the UK housing market will encourage a new level of trust between themselves and the public. Recent You Gov polling confirmed that there is wider scale support from the public for more new homes.[47] By connecting local producers with their local communities, the power of that supply switches from the volume housebuilder to that of the independent developer.

My Dream Scenario

Scott and Becca have been living in one of those draughty lofts in Hackney Wick for the past five years and although the experience has proved wonderful, they agree the time is right for them to now move on. The question is, "Where to and what in?" Becca dreams of a traditional terraced house where she can spend her weekends returning it to its original splendour — restoring old doors, fireplaces and traditional wooden shutters. Scott considers this as pure nostalgia and is convinced that somehow they should be pioneering a future house that would represent better, the way they live now.

After some exhaustive searching of period properties, Scott and Becca discover a new wave of independent developers who seem finally to be speaking their language. Among them are WikiHouse and Pocket Homes whose offering feels closer to their idea of what new homes should be. Keeping their options open, they encounter Solidspace whose interior space made up of different levels, allows for multi-use social spaces and provides more volume for the same quantity of space. The incorporation of split-level units also supports medical evidence that climbing stairs in the home is proven to be an excellent source of cardiovascular exercise and, although both in their 30s, they consider this as a valuable tick to be able to put next to the name.

They are fascinated by Solidspace's Try Before You Buy campaign for their new range of houses. It has represented a breakthrough in house hunting that, once out there, left nobody quite understanding how it hadn't been done before. One of the attractive traits of the brand is its unique multi-level, 'Eat Live Work' internal DNA — employed in all their developments, whether houses or apartments. The website reports a whole series of collaborative, university-assisted research programmes that have demonstrated how their sense of space can be enhanced over the simple, single floor homes. With space now at such a premium and affordability over what they can acquire shrinking, a brand that actually expands the space rather than shrinks it must be a plus.

Scott and Becca's interest lies particularly in the launch of a new Solidspace model called Connect. Along with everybody else in their generation Y, this next step is the most difficult. This unit of 45 square metres (485 square feet), spread over three levels, seems like the only opportunity for them to get a step on the ladder. They can't bear the thought of a fate resigned to those depressing, standardised one-bed units, particularly with all the effort needed to be able to buy anything at all, any money available will have to be begged, borrowed and saved from the family. Luckily, Becca's granny has left them a little nest egg to help put down on their first home.

In the meantime, Paul and Freda, who live in a block overlooking the Connect site are pleasantly surprised to receive an email from the developers in response to their enquiry, inviting them to a discussion about the project. The meeting is well attended, with about eight of the most active members of this tight, local neighbourhood turning up. The developer explains that they are part of a new movement of independent producers who pride themselves on their local connections and the design quality of their developments.

This gives Paul and Freda comfort, especially when they receive a clearly presented book that explains the brand's values, their responsibility pledge to the places where they build, the profile of their customers and some impressive testimonials of living experiences in other projects of theirs. Most importantly for them, there is a detailed checklist that outlines the times the contractors will be on site, when the noisy works will be undertaken and a link to a real-time site camera that reveals activity on site, day by day.

The local developer team seem genuine. They are clearly enthusiasts for making better homes for people to live in, loving their brand, not the usual consultants. They explain that they, along with other producers of gap site development, have been able to increase their delivery of units across London to close to 1,000 a year. A surprising increase in the delivery of new homes when compared with the earlier days when they struggled to get to ten units. Paul and Freda, along with some of the other locals are impressed, more so after John, a neighbour, confirms that on another site his brother has been watching — a development now complete — Solidspace did exactly what they said they would do here.

As Paul and Freda walk out into the clear night air, they wonder how to get themselves into one of these independent producers' projects.

As proper
prices esc:
do tales of
making m

80 Shouldn't we all be developers?

Chapter 5: Money

My Point of View

Our homes dominate discussions around most family dinner tables. On the one hand they are the backdrops to our lives, the places of our fondest memories, where we raise our families and express our personalities. They are where we can enjoy the simple pleasures of protected living, away from the turbulent world outside, watching on as family dramas unfold — this is the pleasure of our homes. On the other hand they are the investment in our future, our nest eggs. They serve the dual purpose as both investment and habitat. They are a uniquely useable investment. This is why we believe that owning a home is such an exciting proposition.

We consider shelter a fundamental right of our humanity. In India, the constitution supports that principle.[48]

Using our own hands to make homes for our families is an instinct inherited from our ancestors that predates civilisation as we know it. Today, in London, where supply and demand economics have driven the average price of a three bedroom house to over £1 million, we have subsumed that human right with other cares.

We are reminded that buying a home will be one of the most important decisions of our lives; often pitched as "the first step on the ladder". We have come to expect its value to rise and all participate in the prediction of a future where we will cash in. Whether or not this is fool's gold depends on when you sell and if, like the proverbial gambler, you leave the table or return to re-invest in the next one. As London property prices escalate so do tales of making money. This encourages the self-interest of existing homeowners who secretly hope that a supply shortage will continue to underwrite their profits. Any support they then offer towards increasing supply, for instance developing on gap sites adjacent to theirs, is understandably counter-intuitive.

Having the money to take part in the whirly gig of London property has always been the challenge. Watching waves of gentrification, I have witnessed neighbourhoods transform from commercial, raw and cheap to sophisticated and unaffordable. As these waves build momentum, the boundaries of fashion extend to new members of the public who would have previously stayed away. It is a flexible and resilient response.

Making then remaking itself has been an intrinsic part of London's historical identity. We observe how with each wave of migration, immigration or change in demographics, districts undergo reinventions expressed by the changing character of their high streets, shops and cafes all espousing an individual identity and cultural message. This fosters in us an idea of occupation of the city for all. This informality, the entrepreneurial inventiveness and the particularly opportunistic nature of development all contribute to its resilience and vitality. Open to trade as a wide and varied marketplace across the full range of different price points is and always has been a vital part of its strength.

The finance committed to development, buying homes or making rental investments is all part of a complex and interconnected mix of money, made up of a combination of equity, debt and other sources of funding. Development is an asset class that is expensive and revolves around money. Saskia Sassen, the urban economist, talks about the poisonous effect of global capitalism as it finds its way to ground, landing like an alien on the best located real estate in London and other cities.[49]

> Property as an asset class is priced by reference to comparative values of other homes in its locality. Thus when global capitalism catapults itself into a street, purchasing a home at any price, that benchmark immediately becomes the new price contour for all its neighbours.

This leaves behind a trail of London neighbourhoods distorted by rich overseas investment, existing residents who have been long-term owners and surviving social housing tenants.

New housing supply should focus on being affordable to the average incomes of the economically vital young Londoners. Both our economy and wider society suffer while this strangulation of supply continues. Without change, London's success, enjoyed by all its citizens, is in jeopardy. The 'oil can man' needs to shift us into a forward gear and change our course from adversity to opportunity.

History and the Current Condition

The relationship between money and property remains the cornerstone of development. When home ownership was widened in the early twentieth century, we had to find the money to pay for houses. We used mortgages that allowed long-term loans to be advanced against the value of the home using a multiplier of the borrower's annual income. The rules were built simply around financial prudence. The maximum mortgage was three times salary and limited to two thirds of the value of the home. The loan was repaid over the 25 year life of the mortgage. Historically this started with the mutual building society, an eighteenth- and nineteenth-century pre-cursor to today's peer-to-peer lending.

The building society members took in deposits that they bundled together and lent out to the borrowers to buy their homes.

Today these rules have been up-ended because house price inflation is now out of step with retail price inflation. Over the last 15 years, annual house price inflation has been running at close to 20 per cent, while retail price inflation was approximately 2 per cent. Over time the margin between these two different trajectories widens. The difference between the two is the amount that every new purchaser requires to be covered by their mortgage. The mortgage requirement rises in step with changing house prices. Today we are informed statistically that instead of a three times salary multiplier, we now require a multiplier of 14 times salary. That widening gap between mortgage and multiplier of income is what has made housing today unaffordable.

In the years leading up to 2008, we paved the way for mortgage instability by changing rules to allow 100 per cent mortgages with no repayment and bigger multipliers of earnings, requiring only self-certification for proof of income. This, fuelled by avaricious bankers and syndication through aggregated loan portfolios on good and bad assets, enhanced this distortion. In simplified terms, I believe that the 2008 collapse of the banking system was directly linked to the global housing market. When over-geared loans met falling values and mortgagors defaulted, the underlying security collapsed. Instead of permitting the banks to follow through with bankruptcies and forcing the securities back out onto the market, they were deemed, "too big to fail". Both US and UK Governments bailed them out with quantitative easing. These soft loans left a legacy of huge national debt as percentages of the GDP for each sovereign state.

We could learn more from the financial example set by the Great Estates who built large parts of what we now cherish in London. They created a financial and legal model of ownership that created a separation between buildings and land. Over 250 years of history, by retaining long-term ownership and granting leaseholds to investors and occupiers, it has served our communities well. We should use a similar set of legal models when developing on public sector land. This would encourage a different set of priorities, ones concentrated on the quality and the supply of new homes rather than the financial speculation in land which we have shown does nothing but feed greed.

I often consider an alternative scenario to the outcome of the 2008 financial disaster. What if the banks had foreclosed on the security that they held in the housebuilders' land banks and placed them into loan default, using the simple mechanism of the value covenant in the loans rather than any long and contentious compulsory purchase public enquiry? That would have forced housebuilders to sell their land banks. It would have created a break-up of their monopoly and an opportunity for new players to emerge. The money that Government paid to the banks could have been used more effectively to purchase these land banks. Government would have ended up owning the land and gaining the benefits of the growing value of the assets on the public balance sheet. This could have kick-started a new generation of housebuilding and created a surge in supply.

It didn't happen and instead the UK has ever larger national debt to service, the bank regulators have reduced the supply of mortgages and the hard pressed wage earner has been punished, leaving huge profits in the hands of the land speculating housebuilder. House prices continue to rise unabated and affordability is now entirely dependent upon the homeowner investing more equity to pay for a new home.[50] The volume housebuilders remain the dominant supplier of all our new homes.[51] Their delivery combines site finding and purchasing with design and manufacturing, but land is their priority. As they work to acquire land, gain consents and build stock, their land banks become the drivers for their company's growth in profitability.

It is not in the commercial interests of the volume housebuilder to build more, build better or invest in design and manufacture. Government, in granting them virtual monopoly over the supply of new homes, sadly backed the wrong horse.

Global demand to invest in property rather than live in it has fed their bottom line. This has been fuelled by overseas cash investors whose currency advantage over average house hunters has allowed them to reap the benefits of investment in the UK with zero capital gains tax liability on their profits. This phenomena has driven the success of sales of apartment blocks developed in London with their identikit range of one and two-bedroom flats bought-to-let and sold predominantly to the Asian market.[52]

Local Authorities have used this frenetic activity to impose additional taxes as part of the costs of development. These taxes, levied through planning, are a combination of affordable housing costs, other Section 106 payments and Community Infrastructure Levy (CIL) costs; all charges designed to help deliver infrastructure and support the development of the local area. The developer funds these from inflation in sales prices; to them it is all part of their costs.

There is a commonly held myth in the public sector that somehow, miraculously, all of these additional costs will be paid for by either a downward adjustment in land price or be taken out of the developer's profit. Neither is true. The price of land is fuelled by speculation and as house prices rise, land prices rise alongside them. The reality of these stealth taxes is that they are classified as project costs and become part of the rising cost of the finished home. Developers have no choice but to agree to additional taxation as part of the cost of gaining planning consent.

This inadvertently becomes a taxation on the supply of new homes. Compare the development of housing to new offices and student housing. In both these cases, most local authorities do not expect developers to provide affordable housing. That type of development is effectively tax free. Supply of both student housing and offices as a consequence has kept pace with demand and although prices have risen, they are closer to the growth in the wider economy. The taxation burden of affordable housing has had a direct effect in reducing supply. I can understand the frustration felt by local communities seeing unreasonable profits being made by the developers of overblown schemes, then demanding that they be locally taxed to give back some money to the same place in the city where the damage was perpetrated. In another culture this might be called blood-money.

There are approximately 24 million private homes in the UK that have benefited from capital gains over the last 20 years.[53] They are mostly exempt from capital gains tax because they are either private residences or overseas owned. The capital gain has been created by house price inflation. The owners did nothing productive to generate that gain. The social responsibility for providing homes for the poor should be shared amongst all homeowners that have profited from these windfall gains. Tax payments are more successful when they have a wider base for collection. Limiting the burden to builders of only new homes is counter-productive when we need a minimum of 250,000 new units annually and yet we only produce 100,000. To increase supply we should ease this tax burden for new housing manufacturers.

Proposition

We want housing available for all levels of income to support London's wider needs. Our 'oil can man' wants simply to ease the levers of control, widening the supply chain of more affordable homes.

The key speculative element in the equation of housing delivery is the land. Land, with its associated costs in central London locations, commands anything between 40 per cent and 60 per cent of the cost of new housing. The conditions that have allowed land trading to become such a dominant, speculative business could be adjusted.

A new public sector initiative to secure gap site parcels of land through the London Land Commission (LLC) would undermine market land speculation and enlist the support of a new brand of independent developers. Operating on small gap sites, with developments of five to 15 units, offers wider choice over funder and developer.

The LLC needs to create their own legal structures for the separation of the land, from the buildings to be built on it. As a result the costs of housing could fall to more affordable levels. Independent developers need help to acquire these land parcels while they take on the risks of planning and other pre-development expenditure.

The LLC is well positioned to offer them gap site opportunities on option-type terms allowing independent producers to reach this first stage.

When looking at development finance, there is always a scale of investment directly linked to the size of the development proposed. Possibilities and innovative structures are made simpler and more credible when funding small projects. Equity investors are beginning to use crowdfunding platforms and could mesh more sympathetically as supporters of individual developers and producers. We already use different arrangements for shared ownership and equity release structured around the ownership of the home. The model of financial arrangements structured around the freehold, head lease and occupational lease used by the Great Estates, would suit crowdfunding and individual investment.

We have swapped a lease structure for a freehold equity structure. Both serve the same purpose: they are financial instruments that permit sub-division of the same piece of real estate or land and building. In recent debate, the private rental sector (PRS) has been identified as a model for build-to-rent with ownership retained by pension funds and similar financial institutions. These institutions could also structure other models of investment, much like a Great Estate landlord, benefitting from a combination of equity share and ground rent. The equity share bringing a share in future values and the ground rent a modest return on the investment cost of the land.

All of these models are explorations of new and innovative ways of funding development that separate the land from the construction and result in lower costs and better homes for the customer — all built on gap sites.

My Dream Scenario

Joe and Declan, two old friends from university, met up for their traditional New Year drink and both discovered that they shared the same frustrations with their work and particularly, the nightmare of finding their own places to live. Joe was an agent working with a national firm on land sales for the NHS and Declan, an architect with one of the bigger firms on a large housing project for a volume housebuilder.

By the time they had ordered their second drink, they had both expressed their woes that, by their mid-30s, they seemed to have hit a brick wall. Declan was not going to make it to the Frank Gehry stakes — his hero — and Joe didn't quite see himself in the same mould as Tony Pidgeley, owner of Berkeley Homes. The more they talked, the more it dawned upon them that they both possessed enough of the basic skills required to be developers themselves and together, they were sure they could do a much better job of it than anything they saw around them. They agreed to meet up at Declan's flat next weekend to see if there was the basis of a business plan here rather than simply that flat feeling in January with the enthusiasm lifted after all that persuasive pub-talk. In the meantime they both agreed to do some more thinking and Joe, remembering his old MBA tutor's remarks, reminded his dreamy architect friend that the plan had to be "robust and focused".

Joe chatted over breakfast the next day with Jane and of course, their two year-old. Jane was a planner and had worked with a housing association but had since taken time off to start the family. Their flat in Hackney, that they had managed to buy, had shot up in value but was so small that a future with more kids planned spelt an inevitable move. She surprised Joe with her positive response.

As they got down to their research on the internet, they found the newly formed LLC was calling for bids from small developers on gap sites of three to five homes and, under the Mayor's Plot Build campaign, was planning to launch 50 new small gap site housing developments this year, across London.

The LLC had acquired the sites from various local authorities having utilised its new powers of compulsory purchase to capture any previously owned local authority land whose owners had traded rather than developed.

The tabloids labelled it the "build it or lose it law".

The freehold of the site would be retained by the LLC who would grant a building agreement to the independent developer and to the new purchasers, a 125 year long lease on the building after construction, paying a small ground rent and retaining a share in the equity representing a small percentage of the value of the completed building. The developers had the advantage of having only to finance the design and construction rather than paying for the land. The new owners gained the benefit of a discounted value of their home whilst the equity was retained by the LLC.

When they met together that next weekend, Declan brought along his partner Claire, a lawyer in a city firm. They had all been surprisingly enthusiastic, despite Jane's rather horror-struck thought that she would be part of a developer set-up, but Declan quoted from the bidding document that this initiative was designed to find new types of independent developer who retained a pride in what they built and whose selection would be based on the quality of the development that they made.

On further examination the four friends realised that, rather than accept the current condition of unattainable housing, they had the skills required to make homes for themselves, sell off the surplus units and all find new careers. The focus was simple — just making new homes that they would all like to live in. As they poured over the long list of detailed entry requirements, they realised, to their amazement that, this New Year thought could lead to a new business for them all, to make their contribution to the future of housing in their own city, London — homes for the way we live now.

We want a
on the wa
but make
a print

94 Shouldn't we all be developers?

Chapter 6: Interiors

Matisse

do with

My Point of View

Our interiors reflect our dreams. Our homes are an image of ourselves. We view from the outside but live inside. We furnish, add paintings, photographs and artefacts collected over time. Each addition carries personal meaning for us and our families. We agonise over the look: the must-haves, the right tones, the lighting, the textures and that precious vintage find that makes things just perfect.

We take pleasure in the reconfiguration of our spaces whether big or small, short and tall, wide and narrow or even some not square. It is all part of an engaging game. We embrace changes to our flexible interiors in contrast to the immovable envelope of the exterior.

We continue to learn about the qualities of domestic architecture — the personal pride and emotion felt when we are in these spaces. Homes in any city: London, Paris, New York or Tokyo, are revealed to show their endless reinvention. Charting the journey of the terraced house reveals historical patterns of social arrangements. Museums exhibit the way people lived then. This informs how we live today. Our understanding of how we, in the past, expressed our individual positions in society, through the interior, is forever widening. We will reconfigure our homes in the best way possible. These reconfigurations follow our dreams for inspiration, but our cheque books for restraint. We hanker for parquet flooring while settling for laminate, we dream of stainless steel kitchens and settle for IKEA. We want a Matisse on the wall, but make do with a print. Industrial-chic creates the warehouse feel with open-plan, big windows and high ceilings. Bourgeois-chic has its fireplaces, drapes, coloured walls and fabrics. Modern-chic has horizontal space, mid-century modern furniture and simple china and cutlery. These are all indicators of our lifestyle choices that change in line with the trends in fashion.

History and the Current Condition

Country houses in Medieval and Tudor times accommodated combinations of our homes and our places of work. Although artefacts, furniture and carpets existed at that date, the idea of the individual home didn't begin until the nineteenth century. Families living exclusively with other immediate family members had been relatively recent. The aristocracy started to own and occupy their city homes so as to establish forms of town-based family life, whilst maintaining their businesses from their country homes and estates. Bath, Edinburgh and London witnessed major development spurts during the Georgian period. Closer proximity to doctors for matters of health, shops for retail therapy and parties for socialising made town-based life an altogether more attractive proposition. As aristocratic families passed succession of their estate to the eldest son, the townhouse became the place where the surviving matriarch could maintain her independent life. At the same time as Jane Austen describes the season, with its life in town for the purpose of finding marriage partners, so too begins our taste for fashionable interiors. The importance of the modish architect, the precise decorative detailing of the salon, the painting on the moulded ceiling and the right craftsman to carve the elaborate marble fireplace all became cultural pointers that established your status and drew on the family bank balances. Historic records and preserved artefacts reveal the splendours on show. Internal plans evolved from an enfilade circulation — room leading to room — to stairs and corridors with groups of rooms that today make up our own private spaces.

A visitor would arrive at the terraced house from the street, note the iron railings and the plain facade, climb a few stone steps then enter through the heavy and ornate front door — painted black.

The stairs, with their use of stone and decorative iron balustrades capped with a carved and turned mahogany handrail, were a good indicator of a resident's wealth in well-made Georgian or Victorian homes. As homes were shared with servants, expressions such as "below stairs" described the semi-basement reached by a plainer stair. This reinforced the social order, whose conventions were subtle yet important symbols of class hierarchies.

Terraced houses have their entrances placed asymmetrically in their elevations while maintaining a symmetrical facade above. This subtle shift is a signifier of English manner differentiated from the grander European symmetrical buildings. The English house has a narrow frontage with simple plan. This drives the design of the facade and makes best use of the internal spaces, with stairs placed to the side against a party wall. In the French 'hotel particulier', the town palaces boast grander doors, symmetrically placed, leading from the street to the inner courtyard where stairs lead to apartments.

The simple narrow house is a particularly English invention. The front door from the street leads the visitor to the first floor drawing room facing the street. This sometimes looks out over a private square, shared by neighbours, offering more social space. A visitor's impression whilst progressing through these spaces was formed by the decorations, panelling, plastered and painted ceilings and marble fireplaces. Bedrooms and servant rooms in the attics were private. If someone from outside the family happened to be visiting your bedroom, it would have been either the family doctor or for purposes where the illicit nature of the occasion brought its own decoration — hence 'boudoir' rather than 'salon'.

Our love of the terraced house reflects 250 years of evolution through continuous usage. We use the word 'patina' to describe the ageing process or perhaps just the pleasure to be had when mounting the stair and noticing the wear on the bottom step — a memory of the many lives the walls have witnessed.

We describe these houses as having their original features if some Victorian fireplaces remain. We have a fondness for personal histories contained within. Living lives, with and without servants, in times of peace and in times of war. Witnessing everything from births to deaths, parties, family celebrations and the daily rituals that fall somewhere in-between. This private home represents an order of our society that is class-based. The same house type was used by upper, middle and lower classes alike; even our prime minister has one at 10 Downing Street. The status of the occupier was defined by interiors with either splendour or simplicity. A perceptive observer could easily determine the class of the occupier and their financial circumstances, from the shabbiness of the aristocracy to the brightness of the nouveau riche.

The domestic interior represents an important part of our social history with the terraced house our most ubiquitous model of good urban housing. As we search for alternatives to provide more homes, this becomes our comparator, our measuring stick against which we will review any future proposition.

Taking a journey through the terraced house offers a brilliant demonstration in scale variation: from the tiny attic bedroom with exposed roof and dormer, to the darker basement with low ceiling heights.

Chapter 6: Interiors

Arrival in the hallway provides a line of sight to the stair. This in turn leads to the first floor, where you appreciate the decorative splendour on entering the high ceilinged salon with its two or three windows and fireplace. The enjoyment of the windows themselves is unavoidable with their dramatic, tall sashes spanning floor to ceiling, framed for emphasis by wooden boxes and complete with shutters that would close against the cold night air while the fire was lit. As well as their aesthetic qualities, a function of the sash windows was to provide a permanent draught to ventilate the open fires and, when faced with the continental, draught-free and warmer apartments, the English would look forward to a return to their naturally ventilated, cooler homes.

Mounting the stair is met with intrigue when reaching the half landing and imagining the spaces that make up the back extension. The changes in size and height add ingenuity to the space inside. Each window inside the home offers experiences different to the next; from the semi-basement with front light creeping in, to the grandeur of the first floor front, to the open aspect of the rear and the generous views of the sky as seen from the attic.

These homes were constructed simply: solid brick walls from two to three bricks thick (9 inches to 13 ½ inches, 225mm to 337mm), wooden floor joists, wooden floorboards, wooden stairs, lathe and plaster ceilings, wood stud walls, wooden sash windows and wooden panelled doors with slate roofs. They provided little in the way of foundation.

Over time different owners have rebuilt, refurbished, removed walls, extended up, dug down, lined with plasterboard, recovered floors, introduced steel, added bathrooms, kitchens, opened up floors and walls, re-roofed, re-pointed brickwork, replaced windows and repainted at different intervals, virtually continuously. This demonstrates the great success of the terraced home is in its endless adaptability.

The recent transformation of the terraced house — from a wartime world of bedsits accommodating several families at once through to the restoration of original features and basement kitchens extended out to back gardens — has now reached a climax with en-suite bathrooms better suited to five-star luxury hotels, open-plan sitting rooms resembling art galleries and multi-level basements big enough to house swimming pools and cinemas.

While these adaptations continue to demonstrate the tremendous flexibility of the terraced house, no expansion of units or accommodation has been added. With demand for very expensive housing continuing unabated, houses that might have been subdivided into two, three or even ten bedsits in the past are now all being turned back into high value single homes.

The terraced house was designed around a social arrangement of big families with staff. This no longer matches the demand for new homes. Current demographics demonstrate the majority of economically active city centre households as being occupied by families without children. Currently, older couples with grown up families and big homes are choosing to stay put. Although willing to downsize, finding a home that retains the sense of space and volume that they have enjoyed for almost a lifetime is scarce. In the last UK census (2011) it was shown that 32 per cent of all households in London were made up of single people, one third of those over the age of 65.[54] This is the social reality of today. We must respond to the changing pattern of household size by generating appropriately sized homes.

Proposition

The design challenge we face is in the invention of new forms of housing on gap sites that emulate the robustness of the terraced house. When we first make a design proposal for the gap site, we create or mould an external envelope to fit volumetrically within the site's constraints — effectively plugging the gap. This generates an internal space or volume, which has been shaped to fit. We use design features on the facade that punctuate rooflines and carve out secret spaces to make balconies. Pop-ups emerge from the roofscape where they can. The whole composition creates a complex geometrical form. The interior grants us more freedom. It is where we can express our own look and feel. We can interpret and plan the space to offer a unique combination of comfort and utility all inside the given shell.

By virtue of closer proximity to their demographic, the independent developer's expertise lies in a highly attuned understanding of their customers wants and a market they know suits their product. The interior they create reflects that personal vision. Interiors are a collection of materials that represent mood, texture and shape. The discipline of dressing the interior successfully is in maintaining a coherent style in all the elements selected. They should come together to surprise and delight.

While aesthetics define the mood, the internal arrangement needs also to satisfy regulatory space standards. These come from another direction, having been developed to ensure new homes are designed for long-term use and can accommodate the changing needs of their occupants over the course of a lifetime. They safeguard minimum sizes. Although welcome in principle, they can impose a degree of control upon the use of available interior that serves more to reduce rather than expand the sense of space.

In a publication that recorded the occupation of public housing projects in Hong Kong, a study was undertaken showing the different flat types.[55] They were all measured at around 35 square metres. Photographic records as well as occupancy levels of the apartments were shown. These were rented to the tenants as open spaces, apart from kitchen and bathroom. The tenants configured interiors to suit their own requirements and although occupancies were dense, the level of personal choice over their interiors was high. While not the UK standard, it demonstrated that 35 square metres suited families from two to five occupants and by granting the freedom over their room layouts, allowed these families a control and personal pride over their own homes that was entirely theirs to determine.

This for me demonstrates that regardless of nationality, humans will conform to size and shape within known variations. Regulations surrounding space standards are less about the ergonomic or physical relationship the human has to space, but more a leftover piece of moral social order where state feels it necessary to intervene in how we should occupy our homes. As a libertarian, I find this something of an intrusion in the way we want to live our lives.

An example of this is in the prescribed width of a door. The door requires two things in space planning: the width of the opening in the wall for door and frame and the space in the room where the door will swing. While big doors herald big occasions, and we celebrate such grand entrances, it is equally apparent that small doors could lead us to more private spaces. These are variations in scale that should be chosen by designers and occupiers and not prescribed by the state.

We embrace the intelligent design approach to the interiors of our cars and railway carriages and want to make them feel as spacious as possible. Open plan space drives a premium for its inherently adaptable offering. In designing our interiors in smaller accommodation, we want to be able to be ingenious; to find ways of making fold-outs, lift-ups and sliding devices that serve the purpose of adaptable habitation.

We would like to have doors that are both big and dramatic or small and intimate. Building in different levels into the interior space promotes a changing eye level, offering different internal and external viewpoints that improve our mood.

We want our spaces to allow for informal get-togethers, places to dream as you set out your novel, edit your movie or just reply to a difficult email. The interior is for living, together or alone, in harmony or in stress, in love and sometimes in pain. It is the most joyful and delightful space that we, the independent developer, can make.

I am reminded of David Rosen, an independent London estate agent who specialises in selling interesting spaces, when he was asked to comment on what makes space feel good. He answered by describing the ratio between the floor area and the height of the space. This became known as Rosen's Ratio and included a star rating score system. His five star rating was afforded to space with height that created a soaring internal volume and his one star rating to that where the same floor space had less generous ceiling heights. This measure better reflects the reality of a human's spatial enjoyment of interiors by rating the volume of the space they occupy and not just the available floor area. The challenge when working within these gap sites should be to make interior volumes that aspire to a five star rating on the Rosen Ratio.

My Dream Scenario

Newlyweds John and Sophie had tracked the Try Before You Buy programme that had become commonplace with all the 'indies' — the independent developers who provided space on a whole new generation of gap sites. They believed that the quality in their product was better understood through occupation and as such, were granting their customers the chance to stay in the new homes before committing to offers. They were proud of the way in which they had configured the interior with ingenious space-saving devices and wanted their customers to experience this first hand.

John and Sophie were keen on trialling Solidspace's latest offering, their Connect apartment model. It was being shown that weekend and they had secured a booking. With this new version, three different levels of interior style were on show. This catered for varying degrees of budget by allowing purchasers to choose between interior fit-out packages or opt for an unfitted shell (unfinished space, which in this case, was a concrete shell). The apartments were sold in both volume and area and were offered as 150 cubic meters, equivalent to 45 square meters of space. The sales catalogue explained the project, its philosophy, the typology, the finish and reassured customers with its authorised five star Rosen Ratio for space.

They arrived at the opening where Kritika, a helpful and understanding assistant, guided them through the different interior fit-out packages on offer. Kritika broke down the costs associated with each option for look and feel. There were options available at a range of price levels, which allowed them to think ahead and understand all the clever moving parts but, most importantly, what they did or didn't need and how that would affect the price.

While Sophie was concentrating on the overall space arrangements surrounding the views across, the placements of the walls and the spaces and connections, John explored the integration of storage options and arrangements for neat fittings on walls, in cupboards and in drawers.

Working with Kritika on their custom design software, the couple were soon gaining a clear picture of what they wanted from their new space and were able to take home a print out of the arrangement. What proved so engaging about the process was the price guide that came with the design — it allowed them to make their own decisions about where they could cut corners, with basic finishes and simple fittings that they could and would change in the future when they had the money to spend.

When John's parents came over for lunch and an update on the house-hunt, the drawing of the apartment fit-out proved a useful aid in explaining how they would make it their own. It helped launch the charm offensive on Dad for the all important help to buy the apartment in the first place. John's mum was so impressed that she immediately asked him to investigate one of the other units on offer to see how their needs, tastes and desires could be configured. It seemed that the same units with their flexible fit-out, were a perfect solution for both size of wallet and age of purchaser.

The inside has parted the outside to forge a relationship

Chapter 7: Materials

My Point of View

I think of building materials as a cook would their ingredients. My senses grow heightened at the sight of timber, bricks, tiles, sacks of cement and sand arriving on site. The smell of wet plaster is always a thrill. There is something that remains childishly exciting about the builder's lorry arriving, loaded down, with such anticipation. We choose our materials for both objective and subjective reasons with performance, quality and patina all playing a part in that selection. Materials are fundamental to the manufacture of our homes. New materials and technologies challenge our thinking and present fresh possibilities for both what we make and how we make it.

I have always questioned the rising cost of new construction and think long and often about how productivity gains could be harnessed. We have explored why land, as a component of housing, is speculative and have made suggestions for the public sector, with the London Land Commission, to help its amelioration.

To better control the costs of construction, it seems we need to make its process less bespoke and more generic. Manufacturing needs repetition. Further investment in innovation and invention will make this possible.

Our building technologies could grow more responsive by rediscovering the very simple art of building. In the past, where the craft of building evolved over years of our making similar structures, it was the process of repetition that made it simpler. We traditionally focused on load bearing structures — tasking walls, floors and roofs to do the job. Whether building in brick, stone or timber, this remained the standard practice for thousands of years. New homes use technology to avoid the occurrence of a 'cold bridge' of heat passing from inside to outside and unnecessarily expending energy. Regulation has established clear guidance for energy savings by insulating external walls and improving the performance of windows. I like to use the analogy of the tea cosy to describe this concept of the external wall's design. It has changed its function from one of solid load bearing, to that of a rain screen — a skin insulated and separated from the structure beneath.

This prompts new design thinking, acting as a revolution in our construction traditions that will create new opportunities in building technology. We are of course used to a long history of evolution and innovation in the employment of new materials in buildings. The modern metropolis exhibits these technologies with steel frames, reinforced concrete, lifts, aluminium extrusions and plastics. I am reminded of the wise words whispered into Benjamin's ear in the film *The Graduate*, where the future of mankind, life and the planet itself are encapsulated by use of the single word, "plastics".

History and the Current Condition

The terraced home has been built consistently from the eighteenth century. Its construction changed very little over that time. Rows of London terraced housing with stone or stucco on the facade and plain brickwork to the rear became the norm. This was called colloquially, "Queen Anne in front" and "Mary Anne behind" (Mary Anne being the generic name for a parlour maid). By the turn of the twentieth century, homes had already installed minimal electrical wiring in conduits, central heating with cast iron radiators and solid fuel boilers.

Firms of contractors consisted of all trades necessary to complete the work. Estimation was based on measuring the work with different rates per cubic foot applied for brickwork, timber panelling and stairs — all factoring towards the final cost. Thomas Cubitt, 1788-1855 the eighteenth-century builder for the Great Estates, maintained his own, London-based joinery works and brick works. These were called the Thames Bank workshops with an area of 11 acres (4.4 hectares) running north from Grosvenor Road to Lupus Street as recorded in Hermione Hobhouse's biography of Thomas Cubitt:

> *The Thames Bank workshops, when completed, astonished contemporaries by their extent and range of processes carried out on the premises. There were brickworks, a large sawmill, smith's shops, mason's shops, plumbers, glaziers, and painters shops, carpenters and joiners shops and an extensive engineering works well equipped with expensive machinery. The size of the works made it possible to break down the traditional processes so that the fullest possible mechanisation could be employed.*[56]

This demonstrates that there was extensive prefabrication occurring at the beginning of the nineteenth century with off-site manufacturing utilising workshop efficiency. In Cubitt's leases, he mandated that tenants use his bricks and his windows. Whilst today we would consider this a restrictive practice, it had the advantage of ensuring uniformity throughout, contributing to the very traits we so cherish and celebrate today in these same surviving buildings.

Building materials and technologies kept on improving throughout the nineteenth and twentieth centuries, seeming continuously to see-saw between prefabrication and manufacturing on site. At each stage performance was improved. Load bearing brickwork, beloved of Victorian contractors and engineers, created buildings with elaborate arches and immensely strong and decorative walls. Cast iron structures were followed by rolled steel joists creating structural frames. Each technological advancement improved efficiency and allowed buildings to grow bigger, taller and stronger.

This continued into the twentieth century with concrete frame structures, prefabrication of building elements, glazed curtain walling and the introduction of mechanical and electrical services providing light, heat and evolving into fully integrated, mechanically conditioned buildings.

In the twenty-first century, as we strive to make our homes carbon neutral, we recall the historical casualties suffered as the inevitable tide of progress washes away their relevance. As camera film was eventually eclipsed by digital technology, so too the sash window, one of the most memorable and important visual emblems of Georgian, Regency, Victorian and Edwardian architecture, slowly disappeared from our homes. Where we have replaced the sash window, we have learned to live with its less elegant equivalent, the UPVC window which, although challenging to our aesthetic sensibilities, provides energy efficiency and acts as a catalyst for similar building technologies to develop. Rain screens are one such technology that allow a separation of the structure from its skin, promoting a new freedom to the architecture.

Housing construction teaches us that advances in technology have conventionally gone alongside traditional design and construction. The ubiquity of the terraced home demonstrates this evolution. The same design principles moved from site to site, adapting in the process, with the benefit of available specialist skills. Carpentry, plumbing, roofing and

<u>bricklaying were all trades made better through a tradition of apprenticeship, investing time in the development of the craft.</u>

Experience was passed from generation to generation. The Japanese follow this craft tradition to such an extent that, to keep it alive, they replace their historic buildings every 40 years. This is the period that one generation of craftsmen can pass their skills on to the next. Their approach to preservation is one invested in the culture of the skill rather than the artefact itself.

Proposition

In finding a material that suits the context of London's conservation areas, we naturally default to brick, whether 'London stock' or 'red rubbers', we do love our bricks. As the backdrop to our lives, we share a comfort in their familiarity. They are the perfect component to suit their traditional role of building load bearing walls. Their continuous ageing process serves only to further their many aesthetic qualities. They are inert to fire, deliver load carrying capability and offer tremendous design flexibility. Like handmade tiles, the particular clay used and the baking represents their locality. They are a small, hand held component of fixed dimension namely 9 x 4.5 x 3 inches (225 x 112 x 75 millimetres).[57] This has made them adaptable. The brick facade is what we imagine our homes to look like in most contexts.

To meet and maintain carbon neutral building, the traditional load bearing construction has changed so that insulation and isolation are now used to separate the external skin from the interior structure, avoiding the occurrence of the cold bridge. The bricks of today are used as a rain screen. They have become simply a veneer, carrying only their own weight.

As a traditionalist, I believe that bricks, losing their load bearing function, have shifted their raison d'etre. They have become the bodywork attached to the chassis of the home and as such, they encourage different architects to fashion their form. We have cladding systems available in timber, ceramics, glass, metal, straw and render, as well as the more traditional brick and stone. The hard work, the function of keeping the rain out, is done by wafer-thin, highly efficient and engineered membranes that are both breathable and waterproof together with the volumes of insulation that sit behind. The rain screen is simply what we look at.

The load-bearing requirement of the building has moved to the inside — I call this the chassis. The build-up of external layers of skin serves to keep out rain and keep in heat — I call this the bodywork. The separation between chassis and bodywork is a new condition for our materials and construction technology. When the inside parted with the outside, an opportunity developed to forge a new relationship.

The cladding is the shell, or carapace, which wraps around an intelligent chassis. These two elements can now function differently: the chassis to form the home and the bodywork to suit the context of the site. The role of the independent developer is to engage with the gap sites. They can choose to default to brickwork or challenge the context with a different material pallet. Their challenge is to present a reflective design that sits comfortably in its surroundings. Managing this approach is at the heart of their task.

The adaptability of the terraced house to its varied site conditions sets a benchmark for our contemporary generic model which must strive to do the same. Each gap site gives the independent developer the freedom and motivation to experiment.

Innovation is achieved through the combination of research and prototyping. I believe that this research should follow the connection between the chassis on the inside with bespoke cladding on the outside. Using this separation as a new approach to construction, we need this research to answer specific areas of study.

We must first answer the question of how our homes should work for us. Equally, how we might form space that keeps up with our demands for flexible lifestyles. How can our space be subdivided to cater for living patterns that have created an ambiguity with the conventional designation of rooms? We want to sleep, work, eat and meet in every part of our home as our mood, the light or season changes. How might we deliver homes intelligent enough to meet with these wants?

We must find solutions to combining off-site prefabrication with on-site works. All buildings must connect to their site with their foundations and drains. Technology can now supply the finished items, be they kitchens or push-fit plumbing; these are skills in the factory rather than on site. We must find ways to introduce the factory-made, repetitive product to the wide variations of the gap site. We need to respond to how we build. Gap sites are invariably small and difficult to access. We will need to deliver factory components that are brought to site for assembly.

Only through experimentation, research and manufacture will we establish the generic form of gap site construction that serves to bring down the costs of construction while increasing the supply of homes. Iteration was the lesson that we learnt from the past, the ability to share knowledge and experience is at the core of achieving our goal. The expansion of the independent developer and the proliferation of gap sites will bring about this wealth of knowledge and experience.

On a personal note, I want to describe my passion for concrete. Concrete is written across my heart. On different sites I am exploring the opportunity to make new concrete structures with on and off-site components. Concrete manufacture is ubiquitous. The ready-mix lorry can reach any site, anywhere and with the assistance of the concrete pump, the wet concrete can be placed in the formwork to form the building. Formwork is endlessly flexible and variable — suitable for any site conditions. Concrete is an homogeneous material that can be moulded to any form or any irregularities of a gap site. Its materiality is well suited to forming spatial volumes and making flexible interiors. Concrete has an economy of means, its cubic content, reinforcement and weight are all known. The act of pouring concrete — filling the cast around the reinforcement cages — has the simplicity of the cake making process, there is no waste, nothing superfluous. Concrete casting requires the mould that when set is removed, or struck, to expose its finished form in the raw. For me concrete is the material of choice for the chassis not the body. The body's form can and should be driven from the context of site.

My Dream Scenario

Samantha had been doing a bit of teaching whilst working as a project architect. She had managed a lot of projects but had grown dissatisfied with both the commercial practice and school. She felt she was missing that essential challenge of the new — that spark of inspiration mustered up from school and one she had hoped would remain over the move from architecture school to private practice.

Shaun was giving a talk on the new wave of independent developers and Samantha was in attendance. She was impressed with what he had to say, convinced by his passion to be involved in every aspect of the project, encompassing a collaborative team of people who worked both on the project and in the wider community where the project was located.

She had discovered a competition being run by the LLC asking applicants to present a new form of home that could be constructed out of any material, provided it was able to demonstrate scalable construction and meet requirements for low carbon output. The brief required a collaborative team effort from a developer and an off-site manufacturer so as to construct an experimental home that would need to be buildable as a prototype. The brief cited "disrupting the status quo to bring innovation to the wider building industry" and "making a sea change on the cost of the unit with manufacturing possibilities" as its main challenges.

Samantha had always found the way we occupy our homes an intriguing source of investigation and had, for some time, been considering the home in terms of chassis and body. This split was interesting as it allowed the facades — the architecture — to meet the confines and disciplines of the site, whilst letting the interior encompass the ideas she had about our different forms of living.

The brief also spoke of the separation between the outside and the inside. The outside looked at context while the inside created the look and feel of the home. Samantha remembered a past office project where they had employed Jan, a specialist in CLT (cross-laminated timber) who swore on it as the next wonder material.

She recalled her chat with Shaun at the end of the talk where he seemed open to anything she wanted to discuss. It seemed at last that her networking might have led her towards a project. She took the plunge, made the call, outlined the competition and to her surprise, Shaun said yes and agreed to meet her later that week for breakfast. The competition site wasn't far from the office. She decided to visit before work the next morning.

Samantha took her sketch book with her and immediately began dreaming up a concept for volume, space and height. It started with different geometries that soon became interlocking volumes that she felt carried a distinctive character, promising an interesting and repetitive form of building.

Over breakfast, she shared her excitement with Shaun who agreed that Jan's manufacturing experience would be essential in understanding and checking how things should fit together. When he appreciated just how different Samantha's ideas were with living volumes, she proposed he respond with some caution, but suggested that this was a perfect project for prototyping and that the 1:1 scale model would allow them all to learn how it might be constructed efficiently, which was after all the point of the brief. Samantha was excited with the challenge and took the rest of the day off work.

Rushing home to try and answer Shaun's queries, she felt elated and alive with the challenge. Out came her books for inspiration as she began to draw. Before realising, it was 2.30 am and the sketching hadn't stopped. The genius solution would have to be delayed while she managed to get some sleep. She'd sparked an idea — that was enough — she knew now that its own self-propelling momentum would see it through.

Our first
of the dev
after they

120 Shouldn't we all be developers?

Chapter 8: The Developer and the State

ghting
loper is
ve gone

My Point of View

Neither the developer nor the state are easily visible. Like hunting in the urban jungle, our first sighting of the developer is in the past, after they've gone. A notice from the state attached to a nearby lamp-post identifies a planning application has been submitted. The developer, after some investigation, is identified as the project promoter. We call our neighbours and share intelligence that the notice refers to that house on the corner and that its redevelopment will be bigger, disruptive, out of character and altogether something that we, the collective community, must try to stop. We all meet in a convenient living room and the feverish activity begins with petitions drafted and emails sent to the planning office. We wait with heavy hearts to hear whether this application will or will not get its consent.

We convince ourselves that somehow there is a conspiracy between the state and the developer to disrupt the status quo. The word "development" has become synonymous with this message. Our first reaction to it has grown to one of distrust made worse only by feelings of helplessness toward its inevitably negative impact on our street and our community.

Were we to think of the developer in the same way as any other supplier or manufacturer, we might view them differently. With most of our goods and services, we find ourselves so intrigued with the latest offering that we queue to buy, rush to eat, or book up to watch. What have developers done to make us react so contemptuously to their efforts? It is a difficult question to answer. The process of making our homes is complex. As we face the growing need for more homes, it is important for us to understand who developers are, what they do and why they do it.

The possibility that a developer might be motivated to make positive contributions to a neighbourhood is derided. They have done nothing to change that belief.

I believe otherwise. The most rewarding projects combine the talents, skills, ideas and enthusiasm of all those engaged. Whether neighbours, planners, designers, salespeople or manufacturers, they should all participate. The constraints on a project, its journey of ups and downs and the hurdles to be jumped, are all part of its narrative and go on to inform the shape the final development will take. The developer is at the centre of this process as both director and producer. The process of development is creative, optimistic and enjoyable. It has parallels to filmmaking and apart from the differences in their digital and physical outputs, the processes in both mediums are aligned. The developer's determination is driven by the desire to see their project become a reality, to be lived in and to be used as part of our cities; playing a positive role in people's lives. To expand on my definition of Development as Art in the Introduction: it is a project where the developer strives for something more than simply profit.

A personal triumph was on a small site we developed in Lambeth, at One Centaur Street. The site had been empty for many years and the adjoining neighbours had planted a row of Leylandii trees on its boundary with the bottom of their garden, fearing development of the vacant site. The building was constructed, awards given and new occupants took over. Several years passed. On returning to the site, I noticed the row of Leylandii trees had been cut down. It was a moment of satisfaction to discover that the neighbours had decided that they preferred to look at the development than to hide it with the tree screen.

We are by now familiar with the shortage of supply and the strength of demand for new homes. Every time we try and find a solution it seems only to worsen rather than improve — the knot ties firmer and the papers fill with yet another series of unfortunate outcomes. London is cluttered with swinging cranes, record sales at £'s per square foot seem to get broken with every posting. Where is our 'man with his oil can'? Development is a local business. In my moments of despair, I sometimes dream of upping-sticks and heading for New York where As-of-Right development prevails and the conservatism we face in making things new and fresh here seems to be different. This is simply a case of the grass being greener elsewhere.

I am convinced that we do not need big plans, we need a concentration and expansion of small-scale gap site building. Independent developers who share a belief in the quality of the projects they make and have a determination to transform the parts of the city that they inhabit.

Nimbys are right to be concerned about their environment, they should expect and deserve to be heard. Development unfortunately, like the proverbial omelette, has to follow the breaking of eggs. Like all forms of independent action and delivery, whether food, film, school or organic supply, the scale is small and focused while the ambition is to change and passionately defend what you believe. With our 'oil can man' approach, dressed in his faded blue boiler suit, let us get to work with a will and find the way. The city can be remade bit by bit, piece by piece to better the lives of wider sections of our fellow Londoners. This is not something that any of us can do alone but, by banding together, identifying ourselves as independent developers, coming out of the shadows and working alongside our neighbours, we will succeed.

History and the Current Condition

The title "developer" didn't really come into usage until the late 1930s. It was associated with new homes that followed new rail or trunk roads out towards the suburbs. Development however goes back to the origins of all our towns and cities. Builder/investor partnerships have always provided the upward and outward expansion of buildings that make up our conurbations. Looking back at the eighteenth-century Great Estates, their landowners wanted to convert their undeveloped land into income without using their own money. The builder was the go-between while the finished houses generated the rent. The builder outlined a development plan and then persuaded the landowner to pay for and provide the infrastructure needed with roads, drainage and sometimes garden squares. The builder found investors who paid him for construction and then rented to families who lived in the houses. The builder took both the risk and the profit, if one materialised, or a loss if not. There were as many failures and bankruptcies in this history as there were successes. Set piece townscapes like Belgrave Square in London, followed a pattern of development stopping and starting over decades whilst their developers went through cycles of profit and loss. We see nothing of this today, rather the finished perfect square. This pattern of patchy development was made whole over many decades through commitment from the landowners to their long-term plan.

This model was used throughout the eighteenth and nineteenth centuries. It was adopted by all landowners, including the Crown. When John Nash, the Prince Regent's architect, conceived of and planned Regent Street, his job, as defined by the Privy Council, included the additional tasks of acquiring existing leases and finding investors. Nash linked Regent's Park in the north to what was the Prince Regent's residence, Carlton House, facing St James' Park. The famous curve close to Piccadilly was reputed to be a way of getting round a particularly difficult ownership problem. There is little difference between this eighteenth-century builder/developer partnership and their twenty-first century equivalent. Both use other people's money or "OPM" as described in the trade, to finance their projects. Long-term investment measured in the Crown and the Great Estates terms in hundreds of years motivates the landowners to safeguard the quality of the developments, preserving their legal interest at the end of the lease.

The Great Fire of London in 1666 destroyed 437 acres (176 hectares) of the city. The Blitz destroyed 225 acres (91 hectares) — almost half that of the 1666 disaster. Both disasters granted opportunities to remake the city at a scale that would serve its immediate needs as well as providing for its inevitable expansion and growth. In the rebuilding of London post-1666, the King and his ministers supported Christopher Wren's masterplan for wholesale redevelopment, only to then overturn their endorsement three days later as the merchants with damaged buildings started to rebuild on their existing plots.[58] The King settled for a more modest set of controls requiring buildings to be constructed from brick and stone with road widening and sewer infrastructure works to take place. In a post-Blitz London, the bombings created the opportunity to plan and rebuild for the future. The state-held powers of compulsory purchase acquired the land parcels. The City Corporation granted planning consents that expanded the supply of housing.

The Barbican development of office, residential, commercial and culture-centre was achieved through the compulsory purchase of 115 acres (46 hectares). This is a snapshot of state intervention allied to private development activity in the city that extended to new towns, slum clearances and council housing infrastructure improvements. Comparing these two state interventions into development, we see Wren's great conception for a planned city dismissed in favour of the individually-led, organic development around more modest parcels of land versus the grander post-war plans becoming less sustainable as development models over time.

The Barbican development is now well regarded which has a lot to do with the quality of the environment, its management, the mixed use and tenure and the long-term commitment from the City Corporation as landlords. Looking at other state-led estate developments of the 1960s and 1970s such as the Aylesbury and Ferrier Estates, we see how these big plans can easily become derelict and desperate parts of the city. The redevelopment of London following the Great Fire of 1666 demonstrated that the individual, plot by plot action and responsibility proved a much better, more reliable and sustainable direction for our future.

I am reminded of Sir Hugh Casson's response to a question posed as to why modern architecture was uncomfortable in its presence against the historic backdrop of the city. He replied that when he looked at a bookshelf holding nothing but matching volumes in Morocco leather bindings, he found it dull, but the excitement of books with different coloured spines, and of different heights and widths, was somehow so much more inviting.

I agree and believe that the introduction of the independent, individual buildings in our wider city blocks can and should give relief and pleasure, the context is robust and the importance of the unusual, the special, the splash of colour and the quirkiness of the new should be fostered and enjoyed.

As numbers of tourists visiting London grew in the 1970s, the development of new hotel bedrooms had not kept pace. The state decided to provide a grant of £1,000 per bedroom. The result was the creation of an additional 20,000 rooms — a 50 per cent increase in supply.[59] This small example demonstrates that the state can provide fine grain intervention to promote its development needs; in this case another imbalance in supply — hotel bed development.

Turning to the developer's motivation, we need to appreciate that the enduring principle of development is capital invested to make financial returns. It doesn't matter whether that is a long-term income stream, patient capital or a profit from a sale. When we read of developers building apartment blocks and selling them off-plan to overseas investors, they sell the entire development, retaining no long-term interest in either land or building. The long-term view held by the eighteenth-century aristocratic landowner no longer exists.

The developer is the producer. They identify development opportunity, manage the process, purchase the land, fund, design, plan, construct and eventually sell. This is a complex journey and I have illustrated each individual facet of the process. The developer will use as little of their own money as possible and will instead demonstrate to third-party investors and funders, the potential financial returns from the completed development. These are measured against other investments and the risks and returns will need to be attractive enough to bring in the cash.

Projects have a difficult life, some even fail to get started as competitors outbid for the site or, when planning is granted, the land value increase is such that the developer's investment partners sell the site, abandon the development and take their profit. Long-term interest in the land — that is the suggested basis for the London Land Commission (LLC) — has a better chance of ensuring projects are developed to completion. A developer's motivation is no different to that of any other commercial enterprise — it is simply profit. Without it, the project couldn't proceed.

The state is the only body that can create regulation and at local or national level, grant planning permission to build. The developer needs that permission to proceed. They work within the regulations and direct their response so as to meet the required standards. This has encouraged a lowest common denominator product to predominate. Developers are unlikely to challenge or improve but rather conform to these standards.

Buildings that aspire to be different, excel or innovate become difficult to approve — they are the exception rather than the rule.

Developers are professional and efficient at what they do. They work hard to bring together resources, investment and skills in a flexible and responsive way to make new homes.

Using the analogy of the restaurant trade, the customer wants to be welcomed and enjoy the experience in a good ambiance. Behind the scenes, a whole host of tasks, activities, responsibilities and dramas have been acted out. The customer doesn't want or need to know. They have their table, the menu and the food and they are out to enjoy themselves. In the world of restaurants, every possible variety exists and at every level from the basic to the Michelin starred. Developers are similar to restaurateurs — from a builder who converts a home into some basic flats, through to makers of towers providing glamorous apartments — they cater for every kind of taste. In my argument, just as in the restaurant analogy, the path to worthwhile and enduring development is through good developers.

The development world accepts the current regulation status quo. It needs the planning approval to continue. We share frustration from it, but accept it as the only way that, as developers, we can receive our consent to build. The local councillors sitting on planning committees and representing their local communities defend planning as a way of controlling developers to an acceptable middle ground. The developers who sit between their investors and the local authority planners use professionals who lead them through the planning maze. To proceed, they just agree to whatever the local authority asks of them. Section 106 payments, affordable housing contributions and the paraphernalia of technical support all add to the developers' costs. When they in turn pass those costs on to the customer and the occupier as a result, the price of homes in London goes on rising and rising. House prices are always measured by comparison with the house next door. If a new development happens in your street and the price is hyped-up to meet these additional costs of planning, all the houses or apartments in that street will, automatically, go up in parallel. The developer and the state are tied together in a dance, where one leads, the other must follow.

Proposition

Independent and small-scale developers are a resource for the making of more homes and have the right skills needed to work on small gap sites.

They should be a natural partner to help the state achieve their aims of making better and more homes. The state should be wary of and review their dependence upon the volume housebuilders. Mass providers of any service or product do not innovate, create excellence or change what they offer. Small, independent developers, that include us all, are able to understand what their customers want. They are flexible enough to tailor their products to the changes being demanded by their customers. They can provide a balance and respond to the variety of demands that frustrate the development of small gap sites in the city.

There is an innate conservatism towards development. An innovative design that individually meets site conditions is different to this conventional approach. Gap sites that are challenged by their locations are more capable of this experimentation. The developer is likely to have more control over the project because of the scale of investment.

To get better buildings, we need to consider a fresh approach to regulation that is more permissive. The role of developer needs to be better understood and gain importance. The rewards that a developer gets from making good buildings should be accolades, recognition, praise and support. The critique of bad developers and bad development should be censure and debate.

Quoting Oliver Marriott's excellent definition from his book *Property Boom*:

The developer is like an impresario. He is the catalyst, the man in the middle who creates nothing himself, maybe has a vague vision and causes others to create things. His raw material is land, and his aim is to take land and improve it with bricks and mortar so that it becomes more useful to somebody else and thus more valuable to him.[60]

I am sometimes asked how to make an iconic building. I reply that a development that strives for its own identity, that is of its own time and that makes its own contribution to its neighbourhood and the lives of its occupants, is a good ambition. In the clichés of marketing speak, we are littered with words like "luxury" and "icon" that we find badged on developments that are exceptional only in their ordinariness.

Development as Art can also be described as a development that is individual and becomes part of our contemporary culture. The best way to explain this is simply to imagine the newspaper arts pages. Turn the pages between articles on fashion, film, art, music and food. Think what these pages are doing to hold our attention. They are helping us become aware of excellence, passion and originality in their respective fields. We should expect new homes to be part of this wider culture; to be judged alongside other arts productions and reviewed in a similar vein. This is unlike the property supplements that review projects tending to demonstrate only what none of us can afford. They show property like pornography, about dreams and make believe — perfect homes, in perfect locations and at impossible prices. It is a constant source of titillation, not of the senses, but of human greed. We are invited to look at a luxurious lifestyle that will, or could be available to us if only we were able to pay the price. Marketing designations in brochures and on hoardings sitting above some ersatz images of 'lifestyle' can never be a substitute for the genuine satisfaction of the well-made project.

When I walk up and down typical local London streets, I can identify the relatively few listed buildings and appreciate the remaining simple, domestic and commercial buildings. Their architectural elements, commonplace when originally constructed, have become a comfortable and familiar background and the whole to which they belong is designated as a conservation area. However at the very same time as we proclaim its virtues, we deny its future. We freeze its history. We are told that making innovative proposals for new buildings in a conservation area or even changing the paint colour on a front door, will serve to harm. I find it difficult to imagine how this is true.

Our cities must be able to change to meet our needs. The fundamental law of the city is to serve its citizens well. The conservation areas and the listed buildings we preserve pre-date our planning regime. They were the results of builders making what they felt served their customers best.

People make the cities they build with intelligence and innovation. Government permits them to build. The result is characterised by three key words: volume, light and character. Developers building beautifully could and should be heroes and those building badly should be villains. Let's encourage the hero and criticise the villain but, above all, bring back the independent developers and set them the task of remaking and intensifying our cities.

We have seen that the state can use powers to help delivery of new homes and, clearly to increase supply, they should. In establishing the LLC they have identified that land is the key component. I have explored, throughout this book, ways in which this agency can evolve to become a vital cog in the supply of land, ensuring that the non-productive land banking undertaken by housebuilders and other land traders is at least stopped on land that is released from public ownership. The LLC can ensure, through legal agreement, that such controls are put in place. With its ongoing activity, the LLC could start to collect data and identify in a positive way, those parts of the city where the gap sites are located. They are likely to be individual parcels but grouped together. The boundaries of these groups could be accurately mapped.

Different strategies are being tested to liberate planning controls for different groups of people from householders and owners of redundant offices, to custom-builders and community trusts. I suggest that more work is done with the mapping of these gap sites and consideration given to them becoming 'liberation' areas. They would be the counterpoint to 'conservation' areas. Their designation would involve their communities in consultation and debate. When designated for liberation, it would be as a result of clear indications that these were parts of the city promoted as places to build. Design criteria, densities and all other controls necessary for development would remain in place, but it would be clear to developer and occupier alike, that this small zone of the city, this domain, would become a place where development was encouraged. The role of the independent developer, as producer within these areas, continues the argument presented throughout this book of good leadership and local connection with an area as the recipe for better quality buildings. Zones of liberation would therefore act as areas designated to help accelerate that supply.

My Dream Scenario

It was one of those professional think tank invitations that arrived in Joanne's inbox from time to time. This one from the new coalition government, having made an election pledge to build 100,000 new homes in each of their five years in office. The first meeting was a round table with an audience of 20 experienced individuals collected from different perspectives across the industry. Her break-out group included Toby, an architect, Pete, an independent developer, and Zach, the internet specialist who had located his start-up in Shoreditch.

The wider group discussion had explored all the different aspects of delivery: garden city extensions, development on the Green Belt, planning relaxation, tax benefits, affordable housing, productivity gains and development on gap sites. Their group had volunteered to look at this last category — the gap site — and what the facilitator had referred to as "The small independent sector".

They all agreed that they needed to get out of the stuffy corporate conference centre and into a less formal environment. Pete nominated a local coffee shop. They each discussed their own experiences with gap sites. Zach immediately pitched in with an analogy from the computer industry. He explained that the history of his industry had been one of disruption to both hardware and software, away from those old IBM mainframe computers with their special rooms and environments — the giants of the industry. He reminded them further that it was the micro-computer, the laptop and now the smart phone that had superseded these dinosaurs. At that moment, they all glanced knowingly at each other and said "Well, why not?" With this intractable problem of housing, could it be as simple as an explosion in the small site, the way the computer industry had exponentially exploded its supply by going small?

Toby, forever the architect, immediately described his love of the Japanese home and out came the narrative around design of small spaces being a perfect experience provided they were designed with skill and a brilliant use of space. Joanne reminded them all just how important space standards were and indeed necessary were they to avoid repeating endless slums. Zach pitched in, telling them that the computer industry was not planned, it sort of just happened in what the biographers called the "garage revolution". Everybody was working away and where some succeeded, others didn't. The one thing that tied together these disruptive moments was their individualism. There wasn't a big strategy; just small invention that somehow migrated into a bigger movement. When the internet was invented, many articles were written trying to understand what its use would be, the thought that it would be at the heart of everything we do was certainly not understood or ever dreamed of.

Zach's reference to the revolution in micro computing had fired them up, they agreed to think over the weekend and meet again. Joanne reviewed the rules stipulating that all proposals needed to define the terms of new partnerships between the private and public sector. When they next met, all their conversations started with the words, "What if..." and gradually, a theme emerged.

Pete reminded them of the difficulties surrounding site purchase, which prompted the question, "Isn't this where the public sector could help?" "What if", he started, "small parcels of publicly owned land were auctioned?" To her surprise, being a planning officer, Joanne added, "What if we identified zones of liberation as opposed to areas of conservation, where some relaxation of the heavier side of planning control could be allowed?" Toby chimed in stating that it would give those designated sites more of an As-of-Right development status just like New York, another of his favourite cities. Joanne expressed her wish that the LLC, by bringing these sites to the market, could banish speculative land trading with which she was all too familiar.

As they drummed up the points of the presentation they would deliver at the next session, they all struggled to find the words to describe their breakthrough. They all looked to Zach, as after all it was his idea, this time knowing there was no "What if", and he said, "Give the power back to the people, shelter is a fundamental human right, free them to make their own homes, help them to make their city the way they want it and from their individual endeavours, a new world will follow".

Centaur S
Zog House
Essex Mev
Stapleton

138 Shouldn't we all be developers?

Chapter 9: Case studies

reet

Mall Road

Centaur Street

Between the viaduct and my dreams

Discovered in a moment, it was love at first sight. High arches sweeping along one side romantically carrying the elevated railway tracks out of Waterloo, and a tapering site between two south London streets. 400 square metres of forgotten land owned by the London Borough of Lambeth.

We bought the site at auction in December 1998 and appointed dRMM architects in January 1999. Our first planning application for six units in a six-storey block was refused in October that same year. We thought about an appeal but compromised instead. The second application, approved in August 2000, was for a five unit scheme over four storeys. We weren't prepared to build the compromise and made a third application, approved in 2000, for a four-storey, four-unit version of the first scheme.

The project was completed in March 2003. It was constructed around three zones: the first zone being 4 metres wide with bathrooms, bedrooms, entrances and a lobby, granting cocoon to the occupier against the viaduct; the second was 2.5 metres wide with the balconies, winter gardens and internal stairs linking levels and kitchens; the third, a double height living space providing user volume. The entire development demonstrates the gap site possibility of bigger units between 120 and 160 square meters equating to a density of 100 units per hectare.

One Centaur Street, 2000

Chapter 9: Case studies 141

The mainline railway viaduct to Waterloo creates the western boundary to this former scrapyard. The surrounding area is characterised by arterial roads that converge towards Westminster Bridge and Waterloo. There is a diverse mix of housing from Victorian terraces, post-war low-rise LCC flats, 1960s and 1970s tower blocks and 1980s pastiche.

The role of the staircase in creating double height spaces is clearly visible here, where a void is created above the kitchen. In addition, the in-situ concrete construction has allowed the half landing level to cantilever over the living and dining area, pulling away from the external wall and creating additional double height space, emphasising the kitchen and dining areas as the hub of the home.

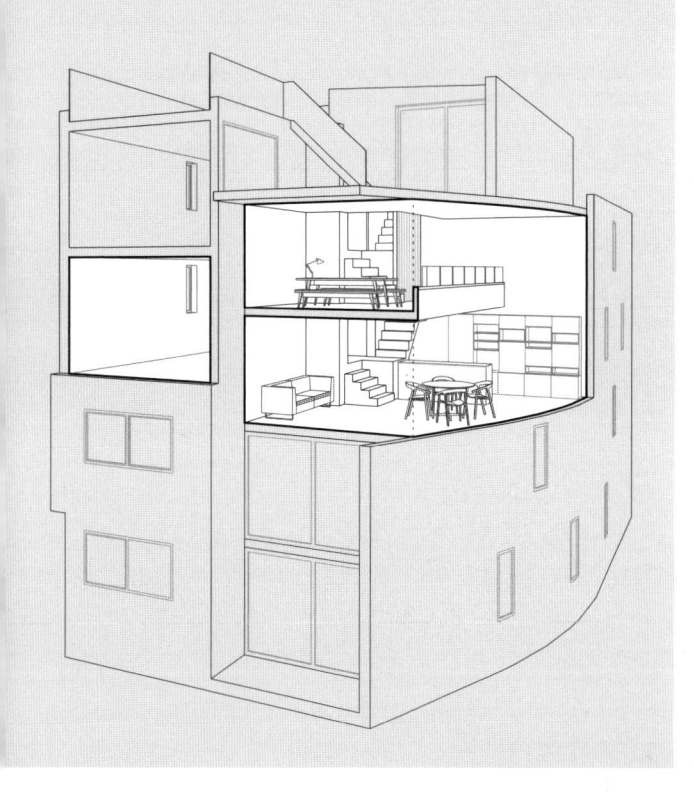

Chapter 9: Case studies

144 Shouldn't we all be developers?

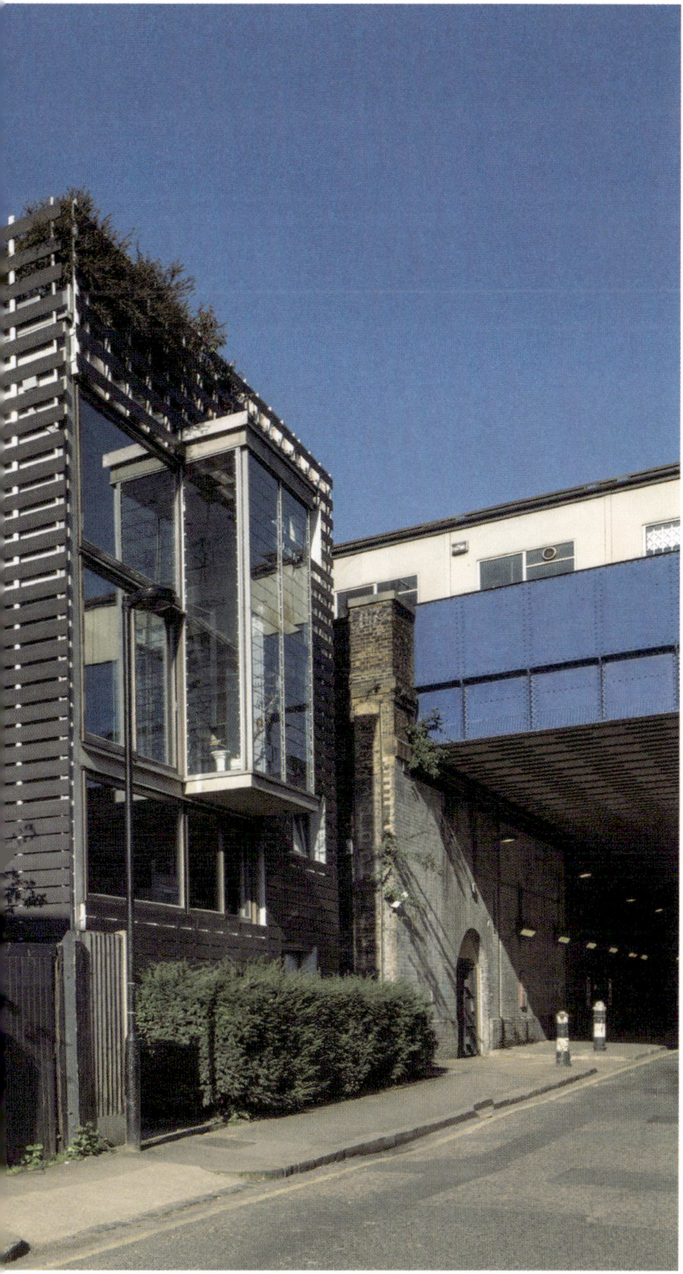

146 Shouldn't we all be developers?

Chapter 9: Case studies 147

Zog House

Home between love and the dream

Our habit of driving around and scouting potential, revealed this site sitting on a quiet residential road in Queens Park. Previously home to six single-storey garages behind 77 Brondesbury Road, constructed in the 1970s as part of its conversion into flats, the site had a history of planning refusals and, frustrated, the owner finally decided to try his luck at auction.

We were fortunate and purchased this 195 square metre site in October 2004, appointing architects Groves Natcheva to design a detached family house of 187 square metres. Planning consent was approved in October 2005, to create a building of two interlocking volumes in both plan and section. It was dug down by half a floor level and, although two storeys internally, its southern facade to the street was only 4.5 metres in height. This met the proscribed light angle from the windows to the rear of neighbouring 77 Brondesbury Road. The northern volume consisted of three storeys (matching 1 Donaldson Road next door), with three levels on basement, ground and first floors.

The entire development demonstrates the gap site possibility of building houses at 187 square metres equating to a density of 52 units per hectare.

Donaldson Road, 2004

Chapter 9: Case studies 149

The site was originally the garden of the adjoining property, used for parking and housed an electricity substation. The neighbourhood is a fine example of London's Victorian and Edwardian northern suburbs, with uniform gridded streets of terraces. Zog House creates a counterpoint to the regular rhythms of these terraces with its simple rectilinear form and white render.

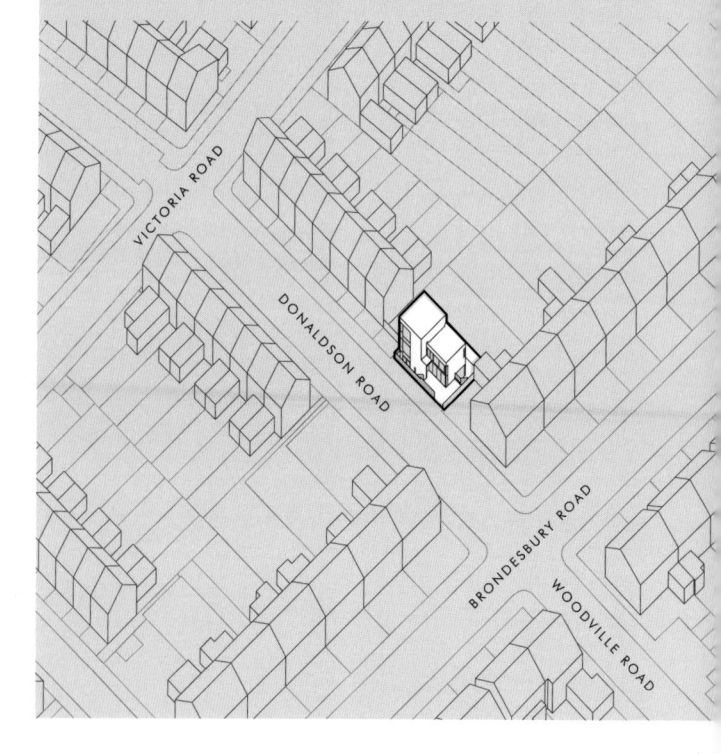

Shouldn't we all be developers?

The generous proportions of the Solidspace DNA in Zog House, allow a triple height void, exposing the section with views to the upper levels of the house, and to the sky, balancing the long views from the living space down to the kitchen/dining area on the lower garden level.

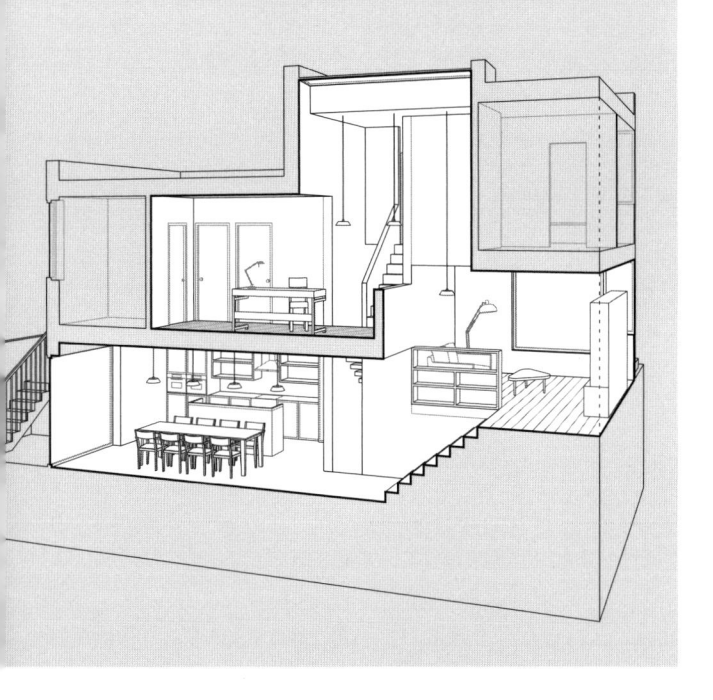

152 Shouldn't we all be developers?

Chapter 9: Case studies   153

154 Shouldn't we all be developers?

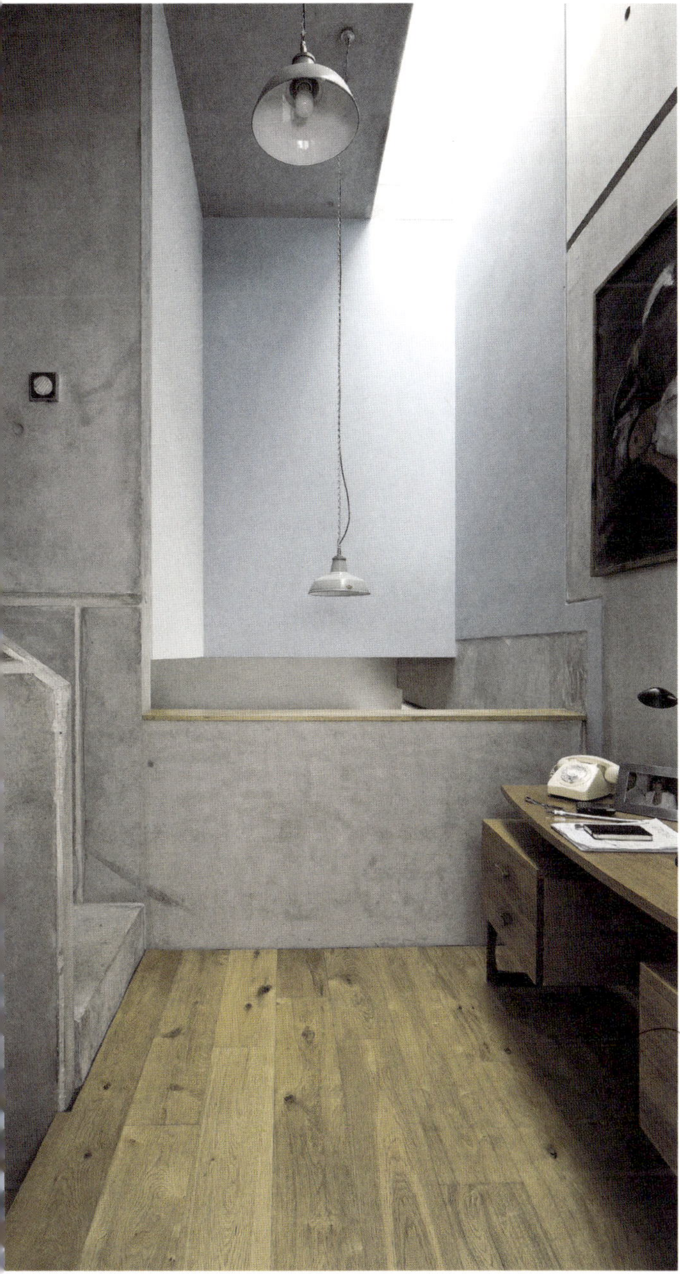

Essex Mews

Forgotten lane to nowhere, dreaming of birdsong

A charming backwater that had been livery stables in a past life, demolished for 11 dilapidated garages and accessed from an unmade lane leading to Central Hill, SE15. The site was an auction purchase made in December 2005, with an existing planning consent for two rather mundane chalet bungalows. An awkward cul-de-sac, we pursued the possibility of acquiring more land to enable access to the adjacent Rockmount Road. This was achieved in June 2007.

A carefully designed scheme of four homes by IDE-Architecture was made reflecting this mews in September 2007. This was refused, as was the subsequent appeal, on the grounds of detraction from the local conservation area, a position we still dispute. Matthew Wood, a new architect, was appointed and the lane connection was abandoned. The houses were reduced from four to three, 119 square metres each. Planning consent was granted in April 2010. Construction completed in 2012.

Three modest, two-storey mews houses were built with their own gardens and featured the Solidspace DNA — the 'Eat Live Work' open social spaces — with three bedrooms above. The sloping site facilitated the split-level arrangement, allowing a dig down and five half levels to be formed within the two-storey, pitched roof house. The facades were brick and arranged at right angles with porches and timber windows. The entire development demonstrates the gap site possibility of building houses of 119 square metres equating to a density of 42 units per hectare. It is worth noting that, had consent been granted for the initially proposed four houses, the site would have been redeveloped at a density of 55 units per hectare.

Essex Mews, 2006

Chapter 9: Case studies   157

This former back land site of run-down garages sits within a sedate south London suburb characterised by detached and semi-detached Victorian houses with some low- to medium-rise 1970s apartments and large open green spaces. The three Solidspace homes adopt the local vernacular and scale of traditional suburban homes, required by the conservation area, with London stock bricks, pitched roofs and chimney stacks.

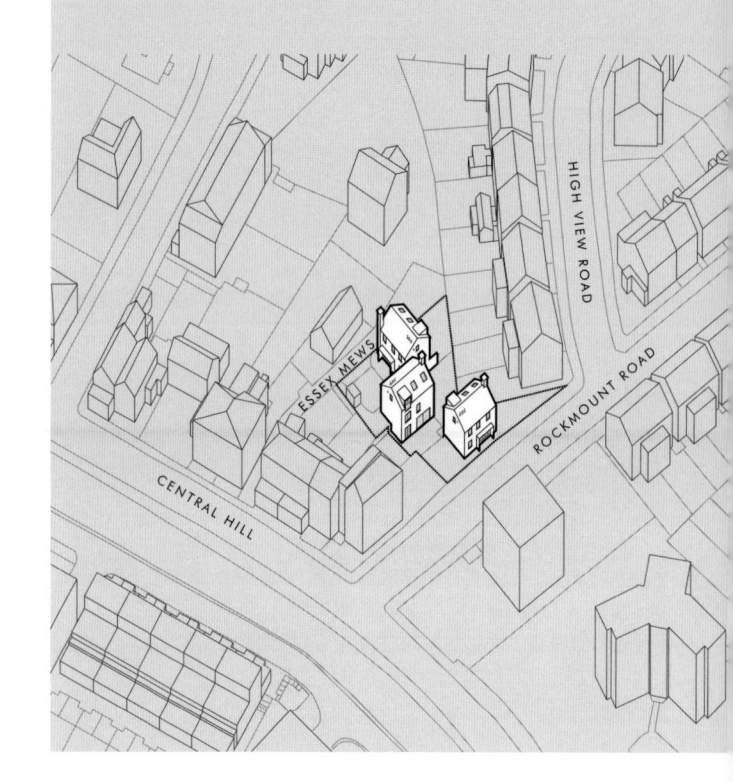

The familiar and traditional exterior belies the invention of the split-level interior. Here the first floor landing has been extended to create a workspace looking over a double height void above the generous dining area and kitchen on the lower ground floor.

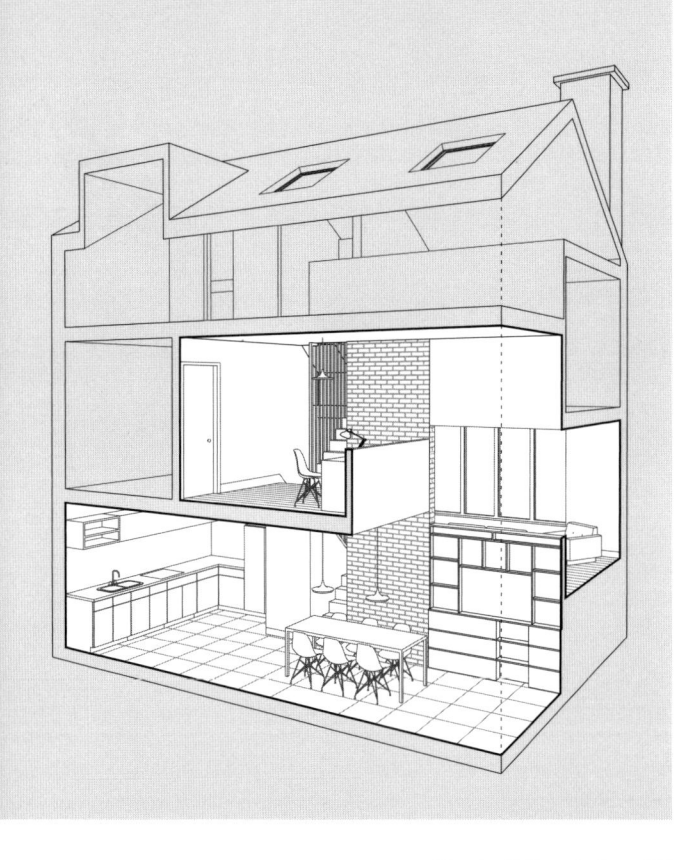

Chapter 9: Case studies

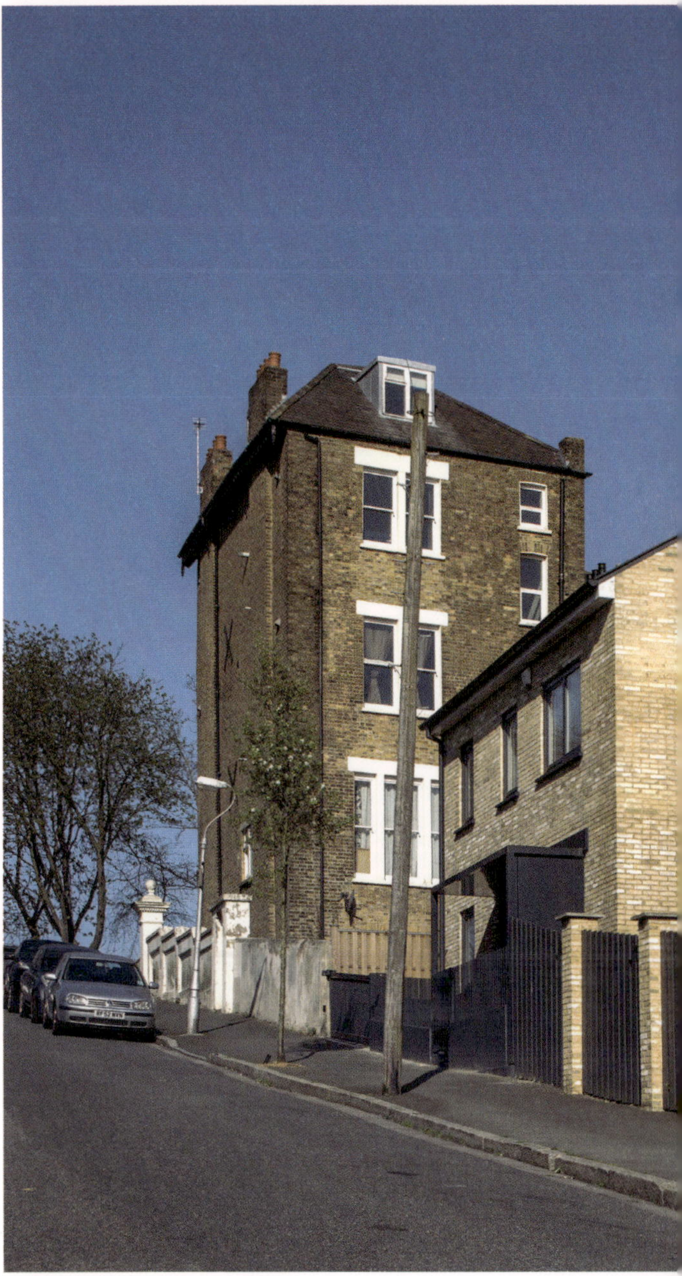

Chapter 9: Case studies 161

162 Shouldn't we all be developers?

Chapter 9: Case studies 163

Stapleton Hall Road

Underneath the arches, dreaming my life away

Sitting in N4 at a road junction, with a faded yellow shop front selling shoes, a single-storey redundant railway shelter and a huge billboard, was an oddly shaped site of 270 square metres. The site, purchased at auction in December 2005, was constrained by railway covenants and a possessory title dispute with the billboard. Long negotiations with Network Rail delayed the first planning consent until March 2009. To secure this consent, two undistinguished houses were the required default. Consent was received and Stephen Taylor, appointed as architect, developed a more ambitious design. Planning officer involvement compromised the consent obtained in January 2011. To achieve a consent that satisfied us, further design development was required with subsequent consents.

Construction commenced in October 2012 and was completed in March 2014. The houses are in a butterfly plan, symmetrical around the axis of the party wall. They are arranged over seven half levels, rising around the stair. The 'Eat Live Work' arrangement occupies the lower three levels, with bedrooms on the remaining floors topped by roof terraces. Three facades are wrapped around by brick, the double order arches reflect the railway arch beyond and perforated concrete coping stones follow the gable to articulate traditional bargeboard detailing. The split-level ground floors create a 'stoop' with steps and two front doors to the street. The height of the houses reach the bottom of the front gable of the neighbouring house, rising to articulate the corner with Lancaster Road. The development demonstrates the possibility of building houses on gap sites between 145 and 155 square metres equating to a density of 72 units per hectare.

Stapleton Hall Road, 2006

Chapter 9: Case studies 165

The original two single-storey buildings were an underwhelming endpoint to this prominent corner location at the intersection of three densely residential streets. The surrounding area is characterised by late Victorian and early Edwardian houses bisected by dominant infrastructure of the 4½ mile elevated Parkland Walk and the cutting of the London Overground railway.

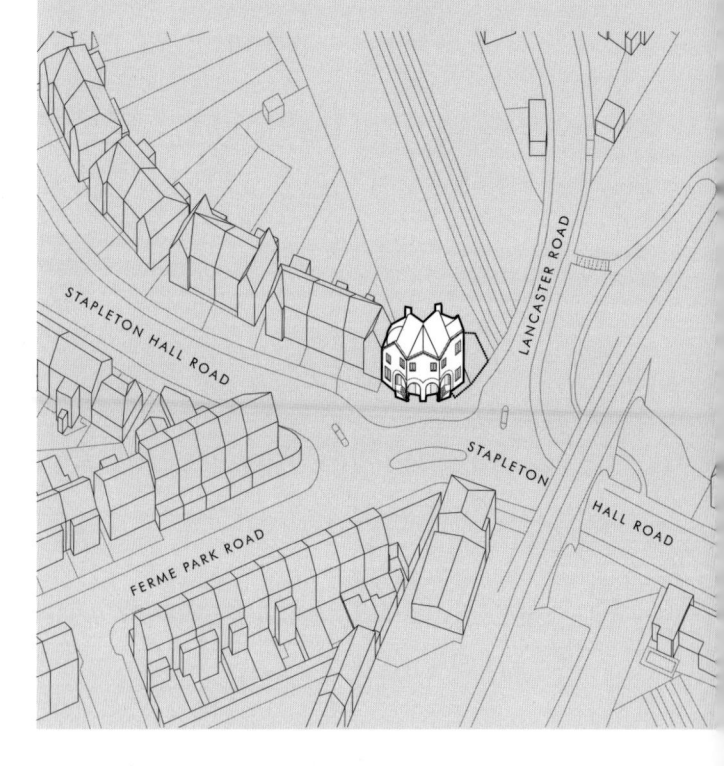

The metre-wide void between the living and dining spaces extends the perception of space allowing both privacy and long internal views.

The two external entrances mean that the 'Eat Live Work' spaces have autonomy from the upper section of the house, where the bedrooms are located.

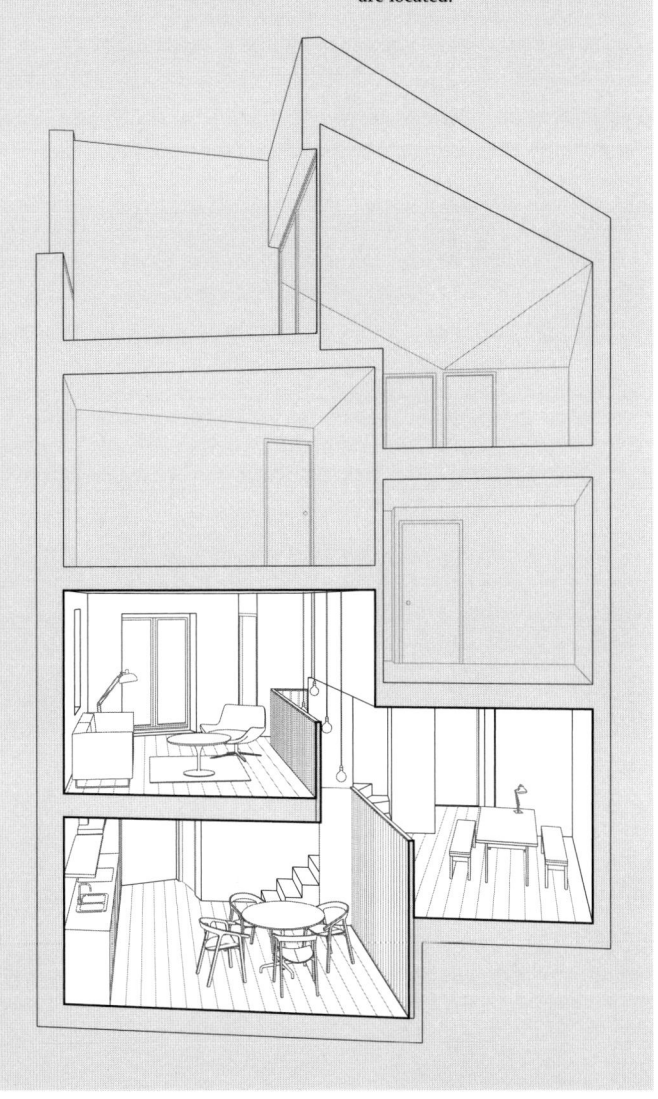

168 Shouldn't we all be developers?

Chapter 9: Case studies 169

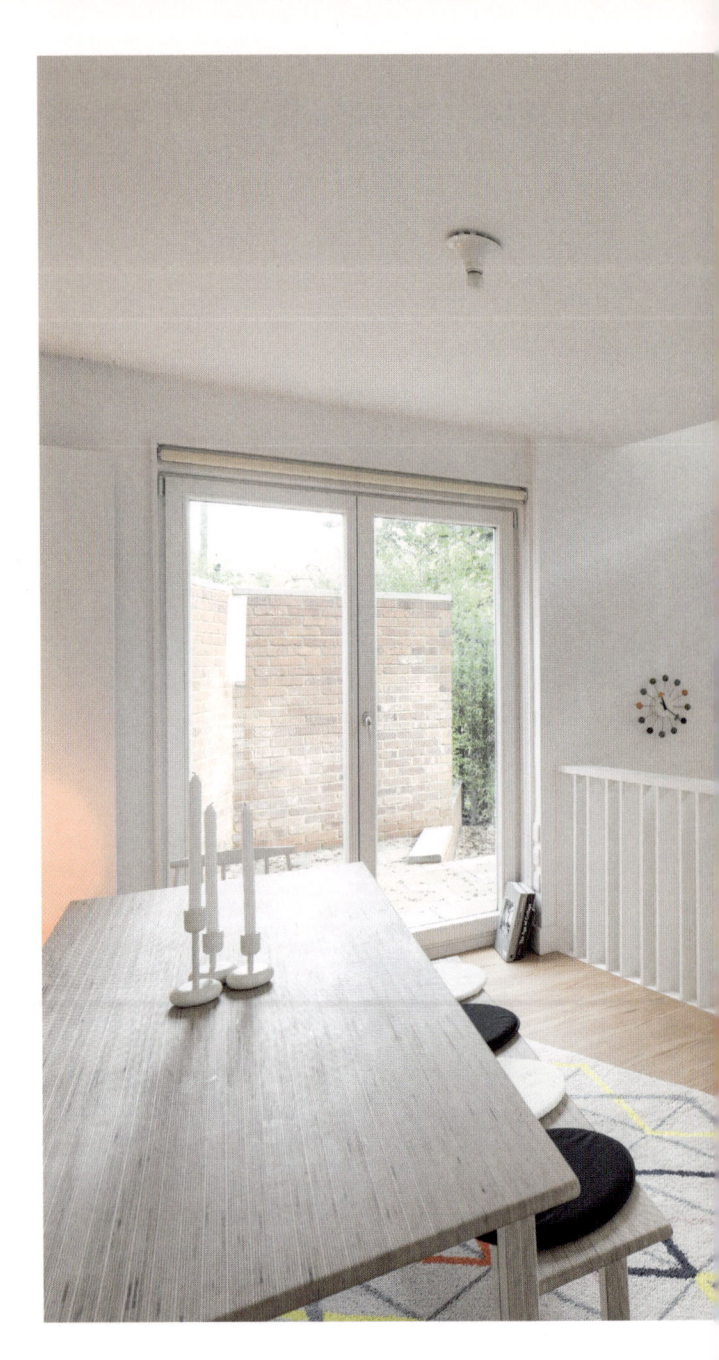

170 Shouldn't we all be developers?

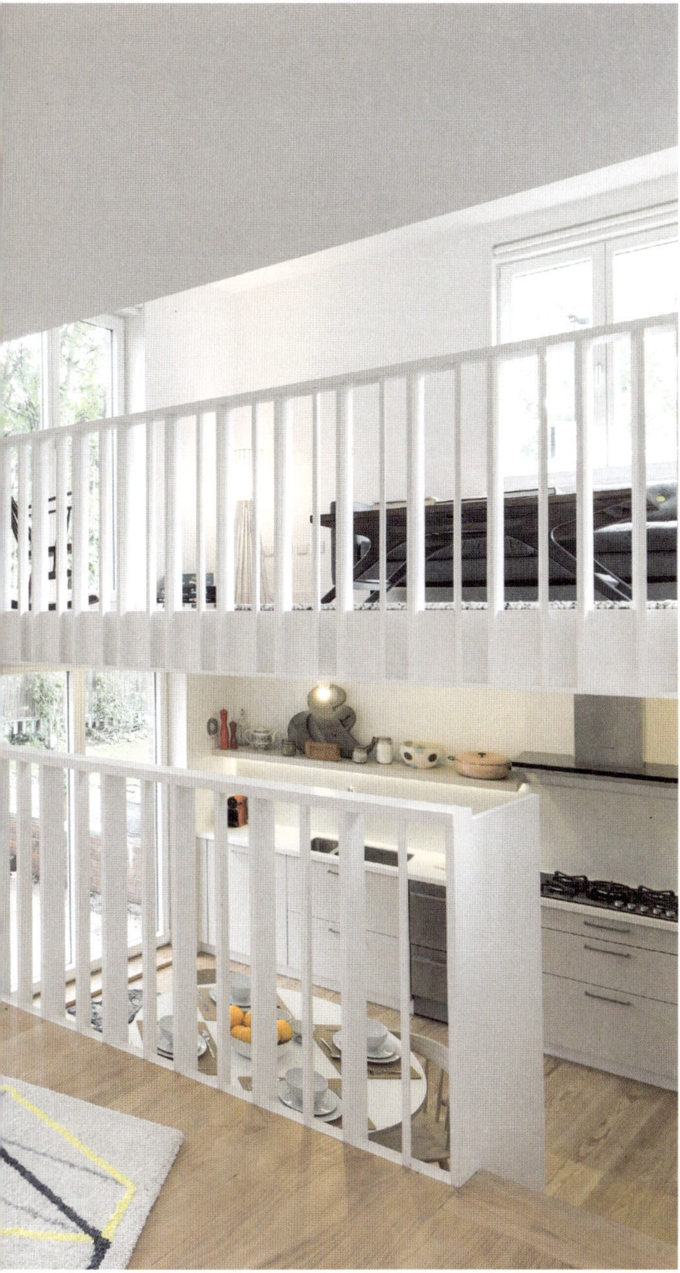

Glossary

Affordable housing gov.uk defines affordable housing as "social rented, affordable rented and intermediate housing, provided to specified eligible households whose needs are not met by the market."[61] This serves the poor and the old and, while the very rich have no problems affording a home, those on average incomes are being neglected. Affordability is something that should be applied to all of our housing market, where professionals can't afford to buy their own home without donations from family.

Affordable housing contributions Under section 106 of the Town and Country Planning Act 1990, local councils can force housing developments to include a proportion of affordable housing in order to gain planning permission: "Any person interested in land in the area of a local planning authority may, by agreement or otherwise, enter into an obligation… (a) restricting the development or use of the land in any specified way; (b) requiring specified operations or activities to be carried out in, on, under or over the land; (c) requiring the land to be used in any specified way; or (d) requiring a sum or sums to be paid to the authority… on a specified date or dates or periodically."[62] I believe this 'tax' on only new housing is counter-productive, pushing up the cost of development and, as the developer's profit margin stays the same, pushing up further the sale price of the homes.

Air rights Air rights grant the owner of a piece of land the right to the space above it, and therefore the right to build up into that space. Air rights apply in some cities in the United States but not in the UK.

Architectural Association School of Architecture (AA) The London architecture school that I attended between 1965 and 1971.

As-of-Right development A site is given permission for development along with a clear set of rules; this allows developers to build without submitting detailed designs and facing subjective decisions. Most developments in New York City are As-of-Right and, if this was to be applied to the gap sites in urban areas of the UK, it would make house building quicker, cheaper and easier, therefore leading to greater supply.

Best value For the disposal of public land, the Local Government Act 1972 states: "Except with the consent of the Secretary of State, a council shall not dispose of land under this section otherwise than by way of a short tenancy, for a consideration less than the **best that can reasonably be obtained**."[63] Local Authorities may think they are getting best value when disposing of land by auctions, but could benefit more by being actively involved in the development of their land beyond its sale.

Bournville A model village near Birmingham, built from 1893 by George Cadbury for his workers at the Cadbury chocolate factory. This is an example in the UK of good quality built housing for the working class.

Capital gains tax gov.uk defines it as "a tax on the profit when you sell (or 'dispose of') something (an 'asset') that's increased in value. It's the gain you make that's taxed, not the amount of money you receive."[64] In the UK, overseas property owners were exempt from capital gains tax but this was changed in 2015, which acts as a step in the right direction for the UK housing market.

City of London Corporation The municipal governing body of the City of London, the financial district at the centre of London.

Community Infrastructure Levy (CIL) The Community Infrastructure Levy is a tax levied by local authorities in England and Wales to help deliver infrastructure to support the development in their area. The tax may be payable on development which creates net additional floor space, where the gross internal area of new build exceeds 100 square metres. That limit does not apply to new houses or flats, and a charge can be levied on a single house or flat of any size, unless it is built by a self builder.

Conservation area Designated areas that are protected for their special architectural or historical significance, and where permission from the Local Authority is required before any changes can be made. I believe the way that conservation areas are artificially frozen in time is unproductive and unnecessary, serving to restrict both the quality and quantity of new building by allowing only bland or imitative developments to be approved.

Cross-laminated timber (CLT) CLT is formed by gluing many layers of timber together. This process creates much larger and stronger members, allowing curved forms, which could be used in finding an up-to-date model for living today. There are already architects experimenting with CLT but it hasn't yet been fully adopted in housing.

Custom build Custom build homes are tailor made for their occupiers. This is in contrast to developments undertaken by volume housebuilders whose design is repeated over and over. Custom build is similar to self build however, where self-builders build and often design their own homes, custom builders employ a design team and builder to work to their brief.

Design-led development see 'Development as Art'.

Development as Art This is an approach to property development that goes beyond that of simply making a profit. If developers have a passion to produce attractive, innovative, good quality projects, the public fear of change in our cities could be reversed.

Enfilade circulation An arrangement of rooms where one rooms leads to the next in a procession. An alternative to arrangements of rooms accessed separately from corridors.

Freehold A freeholder owns the land and any property built on that land outright.

Gap site Small, undeveloped or open plots of land scattered all over our towns and cities. Building on London's gap sites — which are always unique and bring exciting opportunities — could go a long way towards helping to provide the number of new homes needed.

Great Estates The Great Estates are urban areas of London that were owned, inherited and developed by aristocratic families in the eighteenth and nineteenth centuries. These areas include the Mayfair, Portman, Bedford and Grosvenor Estates and today make up some of the most cherished areas of London. We can learn valuable lessons from the way they were successfully developed, as outlined throughout this book.

Greater London Council (GLC) See 'London County Council'.

Green Belt Green Belts are designated areas around cities where urbanisation is prevented. This is mainly to combat urban sprawl. Volume housebuilders try to use this land for development as it is more convenient. However, I believe densification of the cities is a better approach where services are already in place and many gap sites are available.

Ground rent Rent for land paid by a leaseholder to a freeholder.

Homes for Heroes (Homes fit for Heroes) After the Second World War, Prime Minister Lloyd George promised to provide returning soldiers with "Homes fit for Heroes" and pledged to build 500,000 new homes within three years in The Housing Act of 1919.

Housing Association Non-profit organisations that provide low cost housing to those with low incomes or specific needs.

Independent developer A small-scale property developer, who is independent of shareholders and large investors. As an independent developer, Solidspace are motivated to create innovative, interesting and better designed homes. Along with custom-builders and self-builders, independent developers can work at the small scale needed to realise the potential of gap sites.

Infill development The use of vacant land and property in existing urban areas for new development at relatively high densities. See also 'gap site'.

Land bank An accumulation of land for sale or development. Volume housebuilders will build up land banks then delay building to their financial benefit, or sell the land, which has aggravated the housing shortage.

Leasehold A leaseholder owns their property but not the land on which it stands for a fixed term of anything up to 999 years and will usually pay a ground rent to the freeholder.

Listed building A building that is of special interest will be put on the Statutory List of Buildings of Special Architectural or Historic Interest. No alterations to a listed building can be made without listed building consent from the Local Authority. See also 'conservation area'.

Local authority housing see 'public housing'

London County Council (LCC) The LCC was the principal governing body for the County of London between 1889 and 1965. It was replaced by Greater London Council (GLC) to serve a wider area but in 1986, power was devolved to the London Boroughs and other authorities. The LCC and GLC were responsible for some of the most celebrated public housing schemes across London.

London Land Commission (LLC) In February 2015, the Chancellor and Mayor of London set out a six point long-term plan for the capital, including establishing a LLC whose role will be to identify public sector land for development, with the aim of helping London to develop the equivalent of 100 per cent of London's brownfield land by 2025. The intention is for the Commission to develop the country's most comprehensive database of public sector land and play a vital role in tackling London's housing supply challenges.

Not in my backyard (Nimby) This is a mocking expression for the people who selfishly reject development in their own neighbourhood. They often accept that a development or addition — which could be anything from new housing to a wind turbine or rehab centre — is necessary, but would prefer it to be out of their sight and hence, not in their backyard.

Off-plan property A development that has not yet been constructed. Property can often be bought at a lower price off-plan than when construction has begun and therefore appeals to overseas buyers whose interests lie not in occupation but solely in investment.

Patient capital The profit made when investors think long-term rather than looking for quick returns.

Peabody One of London's oldest housing associations. It was established in 1862 by banker George Peabody to improve conditions for the poor.

Polycentric mega-city region A region that is not necessarily defined by continuous urban development but by a high level of dependency or interaction. Peter Hall describes the polycentric mega-city region of London:"By the year 2000...[it was] stretching northwards for some 80 miles from London and south-westwards as far as 110 miles from the capital, it was dominated by the huge built-up mass — about 15 miles in radius — of Greater London".[65]

Product over process The approach to property development that focuses on the end result — the 'product' — rather than the procedure of getting there, including land trading and the long planning procedures — the 'process'. Directing time, money and energy to the product would reduce the cost and improve the quality and beauty of what is built.

Public housing Affordable housing provided by local government. It is regularly called local authority housing or council housing. See also 'affordable housing'.

Push-fit plumbing Plumbing that can be assembled without the use of tools.

Quantitative easing A technique used by governments to stimulate growth in an economy and one employed in the UK during the market crash in 2008. The central bank creates paper or electronic money to buy government bonds which are used to buy other financial assets. This increases the money in the financial system encouraging institutions to lend more which in turn allows people to spend more and increases growth.

Retail price index (RPI) Inflation measured according to the price of common goods and services. Inflation of housing prices in the UK is far above RPI; a study by Shelter in 2014 estimated that if common goods had followed the same rate of inflation as housing since 1971, that four pints of milk would now set you back £10.48.

Rights to light A law in England and Wales that protects the rights to light of a window that has been present for at least 20 years. The law can prevent the creation of any structure that would prevent an acceptable level of light from entering the window, and makes up just one of the numerous restrictions and considerations for new developments.

Section 106 See 'affordable housing contributions'.

Self build See 'custom build'.

Tithe cottages Tithe cottages were houses for the poor in the Middle Ages, paid for with money collected from tithes, mandatory donations collected by the church from every earner.

Traditional contracting The developer employs a design team (architects and engineers) and then gives the construction work to the highest bidder. The design process and the construction process are kept separate. An alternative to this method is 'design-and-build' where the same team carries out both the design and construction.

Type Approval As a developer, you can arrange to have standard designs examined for compliance with the Building Regulations just once and, under the procedures of the Type Approval scheme, this approval is accepted by all other Local Authorities in England and Wales without any further checking, except for site related matters.

Vernacular A style of architecture that is native or traditional to a particular region.

Volume housebuilder Typically public companies that build standardised homes at a large scale. According to Building.co.uk, the top six housebuilders in 2014 were: Barratt, Taylor Wimpey, Persimmon, Berkeley Group, Bellaway and Galliford Try. In 2011/2012, the top 23 housebuilders were responsible for 70 per cent of the homes begun in London.[66]

X-listing A concept introduced by George Ferguson, Mayor of Bristol and a past president of The Royal Institute of British Architects. His proposal suggested that the demolition of x-listed buildings would be encouraged.

[1666 Rebuilding of London Act](#) After the Great Fire of 1666 destroyed
a third of London, the Rebuilding of London Act was passed to
improve the reconstruction of the city. After the fire, the King
and his ministers initially supported a plan by Christopher Wren
for wholesale redevelopment of the city, only to overturn their
decision three days later as individuals began rebuilding on their
own plots throughout the city. The King instead set up modest
controls and regulations in the Rebuilding of London Act, requiring
construction from brick and stone (rather than wood) with
improved infrastructure put in place, such as wider roads and better
sewage systems.

[1909 Housing and Town Planning Act](#) This act required homes be built
to certain standards, which was the first time housing had been
regulated. One of the main changes was preventing 'back-to-back'
houses–terraced houses that shared a rear wall. The act also
required local authorities to introduce systems of town planning.

[1919 Housing Act](#) After the Second World War, under the 'homes for
heroes' initiative, 500,000 new homes in three years were pledged.
Finance was provided to local councils for the construction of
the housing.

[1930 Housing Act](#) A five-year programme was introduced for slum
clearance in designated Improvement Areas. This gave both the need
and the opportunity for new building and development in the cities.

[1947 Town and Country Planning Act](#) This act forms the basis of our
current planning system in the UK. It moved the power from the
landowner to the state and dictated planning permission as required
for development of land.

[1967 Civic Amenities Act](#) The most notable part of this act was the
introduction of conservation areas. See 'conservation area'.

Endnotes

1. Bullock, Steve and Barry Quirk, "Building Belonging", *City villages: more homes, better communities*, Institute for Public Policy Research report, Andrew Adonis and Bill Davies ed, March 2015, p 23. Available at: www.ippr.org/assets/media/publications/pdf/city-villages_Mar2015.pdf

2. Bullock and Quirk, "Building Belonging", *City villages: more homes, better communities*, p 23.

3. Nationwide Building Society, *House Price Index*, report, June 2014, p 1. Available at: www.nationwide.co.uk/~/media/MainSite/documents/about/house-price-index/Jun_2014.pdf

4. Hall, Peter, "London: The Unique City", *City villages: more homes, better communities*, Institute for Public Policy Research report, Andrew Adonis and Bill Davies ed, March 2015, p 41. Available at: www.ippr.org/assets/media/publications/pdf/city-villages_Mar2015.pdf

5. Green, David G, and Daniel Bentley, *Finding Shelter: Overseas investment in the UK housing market*, Institute for the Study of Civil Society report, February 2014, p 4. Available at: www.civitas.org.uk/pdf/FindingShelter.pdf

6. Hall, "London: The Unique City", *City villages: more homes, better communities*, p 41.

7. KPMG in partnership with Shelter, *Building the Homes We Need*, report, 2014 p 4. Available at: www.thehomesweneed.org.uk

8. "The rise and fall of David Lloyd George", *BBC*, accessed, April 2015. www.bbc.co.uk/timelines/zpmhpv4

9. Hicks, Joe, and Grahame Allen, *A Century of Change: Trends in UK statistics since 1900*, House of Commons Library research paper, December 1999, p 12. Available at: www.parliament.uk/business/publications/research/briefing-papers/RP99-111/a-century-of-change-trends-in-uk-statistics-since-1900

10. Jackson, Alan A, *Semi-detached London: Suburban Development, Life and Transport, 1900-1939*, Sydney: Allen & Unwin, 1973.

11. Boyer, Robert et al, *Between Imitation and Innovation: The Transfer and Hybridization of Productive Models in the International Automobile Industry*, UK, Oxford University Press, 1998, p 61. Available at: books.google.co.uk

12. "Profile of the Austin Big Seven", *Austin Seven Owners Club*, 13 September 2006. www.austinsevenownersclub.com/forum/viewtopic.php?t=566

13. "2014 Production Statistics", *OICA*, accessed, April 2015. http://www.oica.net/category/production-statistics/

14. Department for Communities and Local Government, *Table 502: House prices from 1930, annual house price inflation*, UK, from 1970, last updated February, 2011. Available at: www.gov.uk/government/statistical-data-sets/live-tables-on-housing-market-and-house-prices

15 Hicks and Allen, *A Century of Change: Trends in UK statistics since 1900*, p 12.

16 Nationwide Building Society, *Average house prices adjusted for inflation*, 2015. Available at: www.housepricecrash.co.uk/indices-nationwide-national-inflation.php

17 Department for Communities and Local Government, *House Building: December Quarter 2014, England*, report, 19 February 2015, p 1. Available at: https://www.gov.uk/government/collections/house-building-statistics

18 "Chilean Pavilion", *14th International Architecture Exhibition*, Venice, Italy, April–November 2014.

19 United Nations Department of Economic and Social Affairs: Population Division, *World Urbanization Prospects: The 2014 Revision, Highlights*, report, 2014. Available at: esa.un.org/unpd/wup/Highlights/WUP2014-Highlights.pdf

20 "London Underground", *Transport for London*, accessed, April 2015. www.tfl.gov.uk/corporate/about-tfl/culture-and-heritage/londons-transport-a-history/london-underground

21 Thomson, Alex and Peter Wilkes, *Public Land, Public Good*, Localis report, September 2014, p 11. Available at: www.localis.org.uk/images/locj2390_public_land_report_a4_0914_web.pdf

22 Rasmussen, Steen Eiler, London: *The Unique City*, London, UK, Jonathan Cape, 1937, p 224.

23 Rasmussen, *London: The Unique City*, p 228.

24 19 Car. II. c 8, *An Act for rebuilding the City of London*, 1666.

25 C 44, *The Housing and Town Planning Act*, 1909.

26 *Housing Act*, 1930 c 39. Available on request from: The Parliamentary Archives, http://www.parliament.uk/business/publications/parliamentary-archives/

27 Pickford, James, "City's Former Planning Chief on Why London Is 'Unplannable'", *Financial Times*, 14 November 2014. www.ft.com/cms/s/2/5fc42b9e-6670-11e4-8bf6-00144feabdc0.html

28 "Zoning", *NYC Planning*, accessed, January 2015. www.nyc.gov/html/dcp/html/subcats/zoning.shtml

29 HM Treasury, Autumn Statement, 2013. Available at: www.gov.uk/government/publications/autumn-statement-2013-documents

30 Sites with planning permission or under construction can be found on the London Development Database. "London Development Database", *Greater London Authority*, accessed, 12 February 2015. www.london.gov.uk/webmaps/ldd

31 McWilliam, Craig, "The Regeneration Of Great Estates", *City villages: more homes, better communities*, Institute for Public Policy Research report, Andrew Adonis and Bill Davies ed, March 2015, p 76. Available at: www.ippr.org/assets/media/publications/pdf/city-villages_Mar2015.pdf

32   C 71, "Claim to the use of light enjoyed for 20 years", *Prescription Act*, 1832.

33   Thomson and Wilkes, *Public Land, Public Good*, p 11.

34   "Except with the consent of the Secretary of State, a council shall not dispose of land under this section otherwise than by way of a short tenancy, for a consideration less than the best that can reasonably be obtained." C 70, *Local Government Act*, 1972, Section 123.

35   HM Treasury, "Long term economic plan for London announced by Chancellor and Mayor of London", *Gov.co.uk*, 20 February 2015. www.gov.uk/government/news/long-term-economic-plan-for-london-announced-by-chancellor-and-mayor-of-london

36   Emmett, Susan, *Spotlight, Public Land: Unearthing Potential*, Savills World Research Report, 2014, p 2. Available at: pdf.euro.savills.co.uk/uk/residential---other/spotlight-public-land.pdf

37   Rasmussen, *London: The Unique City*, p 296.

38   Rasmussen, *London: The Unique City*, p 202.

39   Buildings less than 30 years old may be listed "only if they are of outstanding quality and under threat". Department for Culture, Media and Sport, *Principles of Selection for Listing Buildings*, March 2010, p 5. Available at: www.gov.uk/government/publications/principles-of-selection-for-listing-buildings

40   Roberts-Hughes, Rebecca, *The case for space: the size of England's new homes*, Royal Institute of British Architects report, September 2011, p 8. Available at: www.architecture.com/files/ribaholdings/policyandinternationalrelations/homewise/caseforspace.pdf

41   Green and Bentley, *Finding Shelter: Overseas investment in the UK housing market*, p 5.

42   Cochrane, Allan, Spatial policy, *urban extensions and volume house-building: lessons from a growth region*, unpublished working paper, accessed, April 2015, p 16.

43   KPMG in partnership with Shelter, *Building the Homes We Need*, p 26.

44   "During the 12 months to June 2012 just over 11,000 homes consented for private sale commenced construction in London (in schemes containing 20+ private sale homes). 70 per cent of these units — roughly 8,300 homes — were commenced by just 23 firms." Molior London Limited for Greater London Authority, *Barriers to Housing Delivery*, report, December 2012, p 33. Available at: www.london.gov.uk/sites/default/files/Barriers%20to%20Housing%20Delivery.pdf

45   Molior London Limited, *Barriers to Housing Delivery*, p 17.

46   Johnson, William, *Lessons from Japan: A comparative study of the market drivers for prefabrication in Japanese and UK private housing development*, report, 2007 p 10.

47 Dahlgreen, Will, "Londoners blame rich foreigners for house price boom", *YouGov*, 10 April, 2014. yougov.co.uk/news/2014/04/10/londoners-blame-rich-foreigners-housing-boom/

48 Housing and Land Rights Network — Habitat International Coalition, *The Human Rights to Adequate Housing and Land in India: Parallel Report Submitted to the Committee on Economic, Social and Cultural Rights*, report, April 2008, p.1. Available at: www.hic-sarp.org/documents/Housing%20and%20Land%20Rights%20Network%20final%201%20may%2008.pdf

49 Sassen, Saskia, "Urbanising Technology", *Electric City*, conference by Urban Age, London, 6-7 December 2012.

50 Nationwide Building Society, *Average house prices adjusted for inflation*, 2015. Available at: www.housepricecrash.co.uk/indices-nationwide-national-inflation.php

51 Molior London Limited, *Barriers to Housing Delivery*, p 33.

52 Green and Bentley, *Finding Shelter: Overseas investment in the UK housing market*, p 5.

53 Department for Communities and Local Government, *Table 102: by tenure, Great Britain (historical series)*, last updated 11 December 2014. Available at: www.gov.uk/government/statistical-data-sets/live-tables-on-dwelling-stock-including-vacants

54 Census Information Scheme, GLA Intelligence, 2011 Census Snapshot: Households and Families, report, December 2012, p 8. Available at: londondatastore-upload.s3.amazonaws.com/g4Q%3D2011-census-snapshot-households-and-families.pdf

55 French, Hilary and Yanki Lee, *Patterns of Living: Hong Kong's High-Rise Communities*, Hong Kong, Viction Workshop Ltd, 2013.

56 Hobhouse, Hermione, *Thomas Cubitt: Master Builder*, London, Macmillan, 1971, p 286.

57 It is believed that bricks made in the north of England were slightly larger as the itinerant bricklayers had larger hands. Today bricks in the UK have standardised measurements.

58 Rasmussen, *London: The Unique City*, p 115.

59 Lickorish, Leonard J, *British Tourism: A Remarkable Story of Growth*, UK, Routledge, p 81.

60 Marriot, Oliver, *Property Boom*, London, Hamilton, 1967, p 24.

61 "Affordable Housing Supply", *Gov.uk*, last updated 20 November 2014. www.gov.uk/government/collections/affordable-housing-supply

62 C 8, *Town and Country Planning Act*, 1990.

63 C 70, *Local Government Act*, 1972.

64 "Capital Gains Tax", *Gov.uk*, last updated 13 February 2015. www.gov.uk/capital-gains-tax/overview

65 Hall, Peter, "London: The Unique City", *City villages: more homes, better communities*, p 42.

66 Molior London Limited, *Barriers to Housing Delivery*, p 33.

Further references

Commission for Architecture and the Built Environment, *Improving the Design of New Housing, What Role for Standards?* Report, 2010. Available at: webarchive.nationalarchives.gov.uk/20110118095356/ http://www.cabe.org.uk/files/improving-the-design-of-new-housing.pdf

Commission for Architecture and the Built Environment, *Improving the Quality of New Housing, Technical background paper*, Report, 2010. Available at: webarchive.nationalarchives.gov.uk/20110118095356/ http://www.cabe.org.uk/files/improving-the-quality-of-new-housing.pdf

Commission for Architecture and the Built Environment, *Mapping Existing Housing Standards*, report, August 2010. Available at: webarchive.nationalarchives.gov.uk/20110118095356/http://www.cabe.org.uk/files/mapping-existing-housing-standards.pdf

Commission for Architecture and the Built Environment, *Mapping Space Standards for the Home*, report, 2010. Available at: webarchive.nationalarchives.gov.uk/20110118095356/http://www.cabe.org.uk/files/mapping-space-standards-for-the-home.pdf

David Beckett, *Trends in the United Kingdom Housing Market*, Office for National Statistics report, 22 September 2014. Available at: www.ons.gov.uk/ons/dcp171766_373513.pdf

Department for Communities and Local Government, *National Planning Policy Framework*, report, March 2012. Available at: www.gov.uk/government/uploads/system/uploads/attachment_data/file/6077/2116950.pdf

Department for Communities and Local Government, *Table P221 Land Use Change: New dwellings by previous land use1, England, 1989 to 2011*, 10 November 2012. Available at: www.gov.uk/government/statistical-data-sets/live-tables-on-land-use-change-statistics

Department for Communities and Local Government, *Technical Consultation on Planning*, report, July 2014. Available at: www.gov.uk/government/uploads/system/uploads/attachment_data/file/339528/Technical_consultation_on_planning.pdf

Emmett, Susan, *Market in Minutes, UK Residential Development Land*, Savills World Research report, November 2014. Available at: pdf.euro.savills.co.uk/residential---other/uk-residential-development-land-nov-2014-.pdf

Good Homes Alliance, *Get Britain Building Good Homes*, report, 2012. Available at: www.goodhomes.org.uk/news/264

Help to Buy, accessed, 12 February, 2015. www.helptobuy.org.uk/

Hills, John, *End and Means: The Future Roles of Social Housing in England*, ESRC Research Centre for Analysis of Social Exclusion report, 2007. Available at: eprints.lse.ac.uk/5568/1/Ends_and_Means_The_future_roles_of_social_housing_in_England_1.pdf

HM Treasury, 2015 Budget, March 2015. Available at: www.gov.uk/government/uploads/system/uploads/attachment_data/file/416331/47881_Budget_2015_PRINT.pdf

HM Treasury, *Implementing a capital gains tax charge on non-residents: consultation*, Report, March 2014. Available at: www.gov.uk/government/consultations/implementing-a-capital-gains-tax-charge-on-non-residents

Hull, Andy, Graeme Cooke and Tony Dolphin, *Build Now or Pay Later? Funding New Housing Supply*, Institute for Public Policy Research report, October 2011. Available at: www.ippr.org/assets/media/images/media/files/publication/2011/10/build-now-pay-later_Oct2011_8116.pdf

London Chamber of Commerce and Industry, *Getting our house in order: The impact of housing undersupply on London businesses*, report, May 2014. Available at: www.londonchamber.co.uk/DocImages/12438.pdf

Office for National Statistics, *Land use statistics (Generalised Land Use Database)*, January 2005. Available at: data.gov.uk/dataset/land_use_statistics_generalised_land_use_database

Prince's Foundation for Building Community, *Housing London, a Mid-Rise Solution*, Report, 2014. Available at: www.housinglondon.org

Stewart, Peter, "Planning Portal, It is harder to gain planning for the interesting than for the mediocre, writes Peter Stewart", *Architects' Journal*, 3 October 2014.

Strutt and Parker, *Housing Futures: Key trends shaping the residential market*, report, 2015. Available at: www.struttandparker.com/publications-and-research/research/housing-futures

Tim Buley, *Public Law Issues in Public Authority Land Disposal: Best Value, State Aid, Procurement*, Landmark Chambers, 9 June 2014. Available at: www.landmarkchambers.co.uk/tim_buley_page_3

UK National Ecosystem Assessment (2011), *The UK National Ecosystem Assessment: Synthesis of the Key Findings*, report, 2011. Available at: uknea.unep-wcmc.org/Resources/tabid/82/Default.aspx

"2014 Production Statistics," *OICA*, accessed, April 2015. www.oica.net/category/production-statistics/

Key Legislation

19 Car. II. c. 8, *An Act for rebuilding the City of London*, 1666
C 8, *Town and Country Planning Act*, 1990
C 9, *Planning (Listed Buildings and Conservation Areas) Act*, 1990
C 44, *The Housing, Town Planning Act*, 1909
C 69, *Civic Amenities Act*, 1967
C 70, *Local Government Act*, 1972
C 71, *Prescription Act*, 1832
Housing Act, 1930 c 39

Articles

Allen, Kate and Jim Pickard, "State sits on enough land to build 2m homes, study finds." *Financial Times*, 18 November 2014, www.ft.com/cms/s/0/f3b76fea-6f22-11e4-b060-00144feabdc0.html

Allen, Kate, "City planner Peter Wynne Rees on the love of his life: London", *Financial Times*, 18 July 2014, www.ft.com/cms/s/2/803fe9ba-0786-11e4-8e62-00144feab7de.html#axzz37zo3XuV8

Booth, Robert, "Labour architect peer says building on greenbelt 'a ridiculous idea'", *The Guardian*, 8 September 2014, www.theguardian.com/society/2014/sep/08/labour-richard-rogers-green-belt

Cadman, Emily, "Housing costs weigh on UK disposable incomes, think-tank finds", *Financial Times*, 15 August 2014, www.ft.com/cms/s/0/a5933c56-23a3-11e4-8e29-00144feabdc0.html#axzz3UPJtPqF3

Chakrabortty, Aditya, "Enfield tears up rules in radical attempt to ease housing problem", *The Guardian*, 1 September 2014. www.theguardian.com/cities/2014/sep/01/enfield-experiment-housing-problem-radical-solution

Cohen, Norma, "Property must respond to changing Britain", *Estates Gazette*, 2 August 2014.

Easton, Mark, "The great myth of urban Britain", *BBC News*, 28 June 2012, www.bbc.co.uk/news/uk-18623096

Federation of Master Builders, "Small sites funding is 'going to the wrong places'", *The Construction Index*, 9 September 2014, www.theconstructionindex.co.uk/news/view/small-sites-funding-going-to-the-wrong-places

Ganesh, Janan, "A world of its own", *Financial Times*, 3 March 2015.

Hill, Dave, "London housing crisis: tackling land banking", *The Guardian*, 2 March 2014. www.theguardian.com/uk-news/davehillblog/2014/mar/02/london-housing-crisis-landbanking

Hilton, Anthony, "How we've lost the plot on housebuilding", *Evening Standard*, 5 March 2015.

Jenkins, Simon, "Set our city free so it can make its own plans for the future", *Evening Standard*, 24 February 2015.

Kaindama, Mujina, "Professionals more worried than poor about city's housing problems", *Evening Standard*, 8 December 2014.

Knight, Julian, "Builders are slammed for putting land trading first", *The Independent*, 28 December 2011, www.independent.co.uk/news/business/news/builders-are-slammed-for-putting-land-trading-first-6282142.html

Moore, Rowan, "Margaret Thatcher began Britain's obsession with property. It's time to end it", *The Observer*, 6 April 2014, www.theguardian.com/society/2014/apr/06/margaret-thatcher-britains-obsession-property-right-to-buy

Murray, Kate, "New York housing supremo: 'The strength of a city is in its diversity'", *The Guardian*, 11 November 2014, www.theguardian.com/society/2014/nov/11/new-york-housing-mayor-alicia-glen-city-london-rental-market

Olcayto, Rory, "The AJ is taking a long, hard look at the state of British house-building", *Architects' Journal*, 16 January 2015.

Pickard, Jim, "Labour plans to force councils to release small building plots", *Financial Times*, 13 January 2014, www.ft.com/cms/s/0/0b74a582-7bac-11e3-84af-00144feabdc0.html#axzz3UPJtPqF3

Preston, Alex, "Room at the top: London's super-prime housing market", *The Guardian*, 6 April 2014, www.theguardian.com/society/2014/apr/06/room-at-top-londons-super-prime-housing-market

Prynn, Jonathan, "London's £3bn ghost mansions: 'Foreign investors are using capital's finest homes as real-life Monopoly pieces'", *Evening Standard*, 14 February 2014, www.standard.co.uk/news/london/londons-3bn-ghost-mansions-foreign-investors-are-using-capitals-finest-homes-as-reallife-monopoly-pieces-9128782.html

Rogers, Richard, "Forget about greenfield sites, build in the cities," *The Guardian*, 15 July 2014, www.theguardian.com/commentisfree/2014/jul/15/greenfield-sites-cities-commuter-central-brownfield-sites

Stewart, Peter, "It's harder to gain planning for the interesting than for the mediocre", *Architects' Journal*, 2 October 2014.

Thomson, Barney and Kiran Stacey, "Tory heavyweights set out vision for London", *Financial Times*, 21-22 February 2015.

Vlessing, Marc, "Carrot and stick approach to solve housing shortage", *Financial Times*, 21 November 2014, www.ft.com/cms/s/0/708549da-70e4-11e4-8113-00144feabdc0.html#axzz3UPJtPqF3

Wolf, Martin, "The sacred cow Cameron must kill", *Financial Times*, January 2015.

"Autumn Statement: Overseas home owners to pay tax on UK property sales", *BBC News*, 5 December 2013, www.bbc.co.uk/news/business-25219129

"Berkeley Homes, Rise of the placemakers", *The Economist*, August 16, 2014.

"Build Bolder", *The Times*, 3 March 2015.

"London's extraordinary demographic rebound", *Financial Times*, 10 January 2015.

"Only audacious measures can solve our broken housing market", *The Observer*, 5 October 2014.

"Rise of the Placemakers", *The Economist*, 16 August 2014.

"The Guardian view on affordable housing: the developers must be made to show their sums," *The Guardian*, 1 January 2015, www.theguardian.com/commentisfree/2015/jan/01/guardian-view-affordable-housing-developers-must-made-show-sums

"Why space standards are a bad thing for the housing crisis", *Building Design*, 6 May 2014.

Acknowledgements

Michael Abrahams – for elegant design
Sophie Abrahams – for penetrating research
Sarah Allan – for encouragement and understanding
which has made this book possible
Luke Flanagan – for creative editing
Duncan McCorquodale – for keeping faith
Andrew Skulina – for beautiful illustrations
Morley Von Sternberg – for perfect photos
Carola Zogolovitch – for patient editing

Photography credits

pp140–141	© Morley von Sternberg
pp144–145	© Morley von Sternberg
pp146–147	© Keith Collie
pp148–149	© Morley von Sternberg
pp152–153	© Morley von Sternberg
pp154–155	© Simon Maxwell
pp156–157	© Morley von Sternberg
pp160–161	© Morley von Sternberg
pp162–163	© The Modern House
pp164–165	© Morley von Sternberg
pp168–169	© Morley von Sternberg
pp170–171	© Dominic French

Index

Affordable housing
affordable housing, 130, 172, 175
Bournville, 20, 173
housing associations, 91, 174, 175
obligation on private sector developers, under section 106, 87, 130, 172, 176
Peabody Trust, 20, 61, 175
social housing, 61, 84
traditional examples of, 20–21
taxation burden on, 87-88

Architecture and design
Architectural Association, 42
architect as chef, 56, 62
architects, 62
as compared to restaurants, 15, 62–63, 129–130
back extensions, 28, 100
Brown, Neave, 61
Casson, Hugh, 127
density, 26
ersatz architecture, 62
Goldfinger, Erno, 61
Krier, Leon, 75
Lasdun, Denys, 61
listed buildings, 35, 61, 64, 132–133, 174
Paris, glass pyramid vs carbuncle, 38–39
Pei, IM, 38
Price, Cedric, 63
Venturi, Robert & Scott Brown, Denise, 38
volume, light, character, 28, 133

Brand
accountability, 71
availability, 76
community of brands, 72
desirability, 70, 76
disrupter of status quo, 71
housing, 71-77
housing brands
  Japan: Muji, Toyota, 76
  UK: Manhattan Loft, Pocket Living, Poundbury, Solidspace, Urban Splash, Yoo, WikiHouse, 75–77
John Lewis Partnership, 69, 71
loyalty to, 70, 71, 73
Poundbury, 75–76
reputation, 70, 76
social responsibility, 76
trust
  between public and producer, 70–72, 75, 77
values, 75

Building costs
current, 110, 116

Cities
context, 59, 62, 114
demographics, UK census 2011, 101
demolition, 10, 63–64, 176
Ferguson, George, 64, 176

Communities
building bridges with, 17, 66, 134
community trusts, 134
nimbyism, 17, 124, 175
public consultation, 134
resistance to change, 17, 32, 38-39
social media, 33, 62
trust towards development, 17, 23, 36, 72, 75, 77

Conservation Areas
alteration, 37
freezing history, 37, 133
Great Estates, 35

Construction
brickwork, 25, 100, 111–115, 126
carbon neutral, 113–114
concrete, 117
Cross Laminated Timber, 118, 173
cold bridge, 111, 114
cost, 49, 66, 110, 112, 116
craft skills, 97, 110
insulation, 114–115
Japan: culture of skill, 114
materials, 17, 58, 102, 110–112, 115
manufactured components, 116-117
new thinking, 111
prefabrication, 112–113, 116
simple building, 98, 110, 132
technology, 110–111, 113, 115–116
traditional methods, 110, 112–115
UPVC, 113

Consumers
commuters, 21
customer feed back, 33
consumer response against corporate suppliers, 72

Developers
as champion, 15
as impresario, 131
Marriott, Oliver *Property Boom*, 131
as restaurateur, 57, 62, 130
supplier or manufacturer, 71, 87, 122, 129-130
building to delight, 34, 64
custom builders, 53, 134, 173
experimenting with building, 20, 27, 115–116, 118, 131
film making, parallels with, 15, 123
heroes, 72, 133
history of, 15, 20–25, 125–130
independent, trust in, 17, 23, 63, 72, 75, 77
Nash, John, 125–126
positive contributions, 10, 26, 33, 59, 123
reaction to, 37–38, 122
reputation, 33
self build movement, 35, 173

Development
Bedford Square, 22
capital invested, 17, 49, 128
collaborative process, 65, 118
conservatism, 17, 124, 131
costs, 82-89, 130
crisis, 14, 18, 25-26
density, 26
development agencies, 53–54, 133
development control, 35–38, 46, 49, 89, 126, 130–131, 133–134, 136
as benefit, positive contribution, 19, 20, 23, 25-26, 33, 66, 123, 127
design-led, 53, 173
demolition, 10, 63–64, 176
fashion, 22, 83, 97, 132
financial returns, 128, 175
imaginative development, 15, 19, 41, 66
independent movement, 19
individual enterprise, 17
infill, 32, 61, 174
keeping pace with demand, 18
live-work studios, 23
location, 21-22, 33, 48, 59, 131–132
Mare Street, 22
negative, 122
opportunities, 15, 19, 22–23, 26, 37, 89, 126
product, 17, 27, 71–75, 102, 105, 116, 131
public distrust, 37, 122
redevelopment, 37, 46, 59, 62-63, 122, 126–127
regeneration, 14, 75
risks, 50, 89, 125, 128

Development as Art
Development as Art, 15
imaginative and beautiful, 41
individual, 59
motivation, 128-129

Development, As-of-Right
rule system, 40, 172
gap sites, 172

Finance / money
as fuel, 17
buying a home, 71, 82, 83
capital gains, 47, 87–88, 173
crowdfunding, 90
freehold, 22, 52, 90, 92, 173
global banking system,
  alternative scenario, 86
  collapse of, 85
  links to housing market, 85
  bank loans, 84-86
  break-up of housebuilders monopoly, 86
investment, 18, 23, 37, 49–50, 73–74, 82–84, 87, 89, 90, 110, 126, 128–129
mortgages, 84
Mutual Building Societies, 84
OPM: other people's money, 126
shareholders in volume builders, 74, 174

Gap sites
gap sites, 15, 19, 20, 58, 89
infill, 32–33
advantages, 33, 36, 39, 53, 58
problems, 116
Mayor's plot build, 91

Great Estates
- landowners, 17, 35, 125–126
- Belgrave Square, 125
- Cubitt, Thomas, 112
- ground rents, 90
- land to income, 125
- legal agreements, 17, 52, 86
- long leases, 49, 52
- rents, 22

Green Belt
- building on, 19, 46
- lobbying government to release, 19, 74
- GLC, 21, 174–175

Housing
- additional on gap sites, 33
- back to back, 35, 176
- crisis of supply, 25
- conversions, 23
- demand, 14, 18–19, 32–33, 37, 53, 73, 82, 87–88
- equity release, 90
- freehold sales, 22
- Georgian, 20, 97–98
- Hong Kong, 103
- Homes Fit For Heroes, 21, 35, 174
- home ownership, 21, 84
- house price, 14, 18, 22, 24, 37, 47, 85–86, 130
- Housing Act 1930, 35, 177
- housing for disadvantaged, 21
- human right, 35, 82, 136
- informal housing, 20, 35, 177
- investment, 82
  - *overseas 18, 74, 84*
- local authority housing, 21, 174–175
- period vs contemporary, 71–72
- private house building, 20–21
- property as pornography, 132
- public housing programmes, 20
- rationing, 14
- rich and poor, 20-21
- semi-detached, 20, 59-60
- shared ownership, 90
- social housing, 61, 84
- styles, 34, 60, 61
- suburban, 21–22
- urban housing in UK, 60
- Victorian, 20, 98-99

Interiors
- historic, 97–99
- internal volumes, 15, 28, 104, 117
- lifestyle choices, 96–97
- open plan space, 96, 101
- regulatory space standards, 102-103
- social arrangements 96, 101
- social history, 99
- stair, 27–28, 62, 98–100, 112
  - *half-landing,* 28, 100
  - *back extension,* 28, 100
- status, 97–99
- shell, 102, 115

Investment
- asset, 18, 82, 84
- overseas, 18, 27, 74, 87
- speculation gain, 88

Japan
- craft tradition, 114
- housing brand, 76

Land
- added value with consent, 50
- agricultural, 21
- air rights, 48, 172
- compulsory purchase, 126
- Domesday Book, 48
- English land law, 48, 172
- existing plots, 26, 126
- disposal by local authorities, 51
  - *by auction, public tender,* 51
- disposals by public sector, 52–54, 172
- financial speculation in, 86
- fundamental, 26
- holdings by local authorities, 26, 51
- inner-city, 46
- land banks, 86–87, 133, 174
- landowners, 17, 46, 48, 51, 125-126, 177
  - *responsibility on to state,* 22, 35
  - *long term investments,* 125
- land parcels, 48, 52–53, 89, 126–127, 133
- land receipt on completion, 53
- liberation areas, 134
- London Land Commission, 52–55, 89, 110, 129, 133, 175
- long leases, 22, 49, 52
- Metro Land, 21

New Town Corporations, 53
ownership, 47–48, 52, 54, 126
 control, leasing, selling, 46, 86
partnering arrangements, 52
railways, 15, 21, 25, 46
redundant urban, 26, 51
sites with consents, 47
speculation in, 86, 89
supply of, 46-47, 52, 73
trading in, 47, 51–54
transferable rights, 46, 48

London

Blitz, 20, 126
City Corporation, 126–127
composition of households, 101
economic vitality, 33
global free trade, 25
Great Fire of London 1666, 25, 34, 126-127, 176
 building laws 1667, 34, 126, 176
 planned city, 126
 planned city, 126
 Wren, Christopher, 126
growth of, 14, 126
immigration, 83
 as trigger for change, 83
 re-invention of districts, 83
intervention by state, 16, 126, 128
 Barbican development, 127
 compulsory purchase, 86, 91, 126–127
LLC, see under land
LCC, 21, 174
Metropolitan Board of Works, est 1855
 Bazelgette, Joseph, Chief Engineer, 34
 Great Stink, 1858, 34
Post war construction, 20-21, 127
 Public and private, 25
Rasmussen, Steen Eiler
 London, the Unique City, author, 27, 60

Planning

basement extensions, 38, 101
context, 39, 128
CIL, 87, 173
current planning system
 origins of, 32, 177
design, 17, 36, 38–40, 42, 131, 134
 no alteration to, 36
listed buildings, 35, 61, 64, 132–133, 174
minor applications, 39
New York, 40, 48, 124, 172
permissive, 131
planning permission, 16–17, 21, 129
prescriptive, 26
Rees, Peter Wynne, 36
regulation of buildings 1667, 176
regulations, easing of, 10, 39, 103, 131
resistance to change, 17, 32
Section 106, 87, 130, 172, 176
Town and Country Planning Act
 1947, 21, 34, 177
 1990, 172
status quo, 16, 19, 34, 122, 130,
taxation on supply, 88
unsatisfactory buildings, 38

Regulation

easing of, 10, 39, 103, 131
fresh approach to planning permission, 20, 131
State, role of, 35, 103, 127–128, 133

Solidspace

as brand, 65, 77
Connect apartment, 78, 105
demonstrates Development as Art, 27
half level arrangement, 28, 42, 77-78, 156, 164
the solid, 15
the void, 15, 143, 151, 167
split section, 77, 156, 159, 164
Try Before You Buy, 78
volume, 15, 28, 77, 105

The terraced house

adaptability of, 60–61, 101, 115
as brand, 60
British invention, 60
class based society, 98–99
construction of, 100, 111
Downing Street, 99
party wall, 98
transformation of, 101

Values

affordability, 37, 83–86, 89, 172
  equity share, 90
bricks and mortar as investment, 18, 131
building consent gives value, 50
capital gains, 47, 173
house price inflation, 18, 24, 47, 85, 87–88, 175
RPI (Retail Price Index), 24, 175
Rosen, David (Rosen's Ratio), 104-105
scarcity, 73
  drives up prices, 74

Volume housebuilders

as break on supply, 74
brands, lack of, 71, 73
buying and holding of land, 47, 73, 86-87, 89, 133
land, 19, 46, 73-74
  as priority, 74, 87
luxury lifestyle, 73
profitability, by constraining supply, 74
shareholders, 74, 174
state, dependence, 131
supply dominated by, 87